Secret Sisters

by

Tristi Pinkston

Valor Publishing Group, LLC

This is a work of fiction, and the views expressed herein are the sole responsibility of the author. Likewise, characters, places, and incidents are either the product of the author's imagination or are represented fictitiously, and any resemblance to actual persons, living or dead, or actual events or locales, is entirely coincidental.

Secret Sisters

Published by Valor Publishing Group, LLC
P.O. Box 2516
Orem, Utah 84059-2516

Hardcover edition ISBN: 978-1-935546-09-2

Printed in the United States of America
Year of first printing: 2010

10 9 8 7 6 5 4 3 2 1

For my husband, Matt.
Thank you for all your support
and for your dedication to me.
I love you.

Endorsements

As a crusty old broad myself, I have no trouble recognizing another woman who qualifies, and Ida Mae Babbitt definitely does. As Relief Society President, she steams ahead in her pursuit of what is right, even when it means breaking the law and facing a stint in the cooler. Her counselors, Arlette and Tansy, are swept along in her wake, and a more unconventional but creative trio would be hard to imagine, especially when they face the bad guys armed with only a heavy skillet and knitting needles. It's a twisting road Tristi Pinkston takes the reader on, but it's worth the trip.

— Lael Littke, author of The Company of Good Women Series

Give me a heroine who can wield the Spirit and a frying pan with equal nerve! That's my kind of Crusty Old Broad. Tristi Pinkston adds a dose of mystery and some down-home humor to create a recipe for fun.

— Nancy Anderson, author of The Company of Good Women Series

In my three years as Education counselor and my three years as Relief Society president, I never had this much fun. What a clever story. Once I started reading, I didn't want to close the lid to my laptop. Each one of the characters came alive in my mind as I was taken on a very unusual Relief Society presidency adventure. It was one filled with humor and suspense that I will long remember.

— JoAnn Arnold, author of *The Silent Patriots*

Acknowledgements

There are so many people to thank—I feel truly blessed to have so many friends who cheer me on.

First, my husband, Matt, who stayed up late with me one night to brainstorm this plot. We were giggling, it was silly—and it was one of the most fun nights of my life.

My children: Caryn, Ammon, Joseph, and Benjamin—I know it's hard when I'm on the computer and you can't use it. Thanks for being patient, and yes, I do still plan to get more memory for the kids' computer.

BJ, Candace, Muriel, and Cash—you guys are not only responsible for taking this book to print, but you are some of my dearest friends. I couldn't ask for a more wonderful publisher or more awesome friends.

A huge thank you to Keith, Kim, Heather, and Nichole—this was the first book I brought when we started our critique group, and you guys were right by my side through the whole process. Thank you for being my friends and for pointing out those little things I just don't see. The saying is definitely true—you can't edit yourself. Also a thank you to the LDStorymakers online critique group for your help.

Thank you to the LDStorymakers, my family of writers. You're a foundation and a backbone for me in all that I do, not just writing.

Last but not least, thank you to Ida Mae, Arlette, Tansy, Ren, and Eden. Thank you for popping into my head and talking to me. You've brought a lot of joy into my life, and I can't wait to see what you'll be up to next.

*The persons depicted in this book
are professional fictional characters.*

Do not try this at home.

Chapter 1

Ida Mae Babbitt didn't know what cookie to serve with bad news. She pulled out a dish and arranged three different varieties on it, then straightened the doily on the back of her sofa. Not a cobweb, not a speck of dust, not one thing out of place—everything was perfect, as it always was. Chaos simply was not allowed in Ida Mae's immaculate world.

She looked at the clock. It was nine on the dot, and still the members of her presidency hadn't arrived. She took a deep breath, reminding herself of her New Year's Resolution to stop being critical. Not everyone had her internal clock or built-in aversion to being late. When she heard the footsteps on her porch a few minutes later, however, she had to paste a smile on her face. It wouldn't do any good to start off the meeting with a sour attitude.

The ladies filed in and sat down, a carbon copy of the seats they had occupied at last week's presidency meeting. Arlette Morgan, the first counselor, sat in the rocking chair. Tansy Smith, the second counselor, sat on one end of the sofa, while Hannah Eyre, the secretary, took the other end. Hannah was by far the youngest of the bunch at twenty-eight—the remaining women were a little closer to Ida Mae's age. Experience, she always said, beats out energy any day. But she was glad for Hannah's vitality. Most days, Ida Mae agreed with the old saying, her "get-up-and-go got up and left."

"Thank you for coming," Ida Mae greeted after Tansy's quick, yet sincere, opening prayer. "We've got quite a bit to discuss today. Before we get into all the regular business, I do think there's something you should know." She took off her reading glasses, which she really didn't need, and made the pretense of polishing them, although what she wanted was to stall for time. She hated this part of her job—imparting bad news, trying to find ways to help and not really knowing how. It wasn't always about new babies or new move-ins.

"Bishop Sylvester told me, in confidence, that his doctor has recommended he slow things down a bit. He's been having problems with his blood pressure, and if he doesn't take some stress off, the doctor is afraid he may have a stroke."

Tansy gasped. "They won't release that dear man, will they? We haven't had such a good bishop since . . . well, I can't remember when."

Ida Mae shook her head. "I certainly hope not, Tansy. I agree with you—he may be a young thing, but he's got a head on his shoulders." She stopped to mentally calculate the bishop's age. He was forty-five. Where she came from, that was definitely young.

"There's more," she continued. "His wife, as you know, is in a family way. They thought they were having twins, but they were told last week that she's going to have triplets."

"Mercy!" Tansy sat forward. "Triplets? On top of the four they already have? No wonder the poor man is having blood pressure problems."

"I think it's more likely Sister Sylvester is the one having blood pressure problems," Arlette said. "He's hardly ever home. She's the one dealing with the four little ones, plus the pregnancy."

Ida Mae secretly agreed, but, remembering her pledge, spoke up. "Now, we don't know what goes on in their home, and it's not our place to judge. Our place is to support the bishop in any way we can. I've been giving it a lot of thought, and I think we should try to take care of as much ward business as we can without troubling him." She lifted a hand slightly against the objection she knew Arlette was about to raise. "Now, I'm not saying we're going to keep anything important from him. I just think if something comes up, and we *can* handle it ourselves, well, we *ought* to."

Tansy nodded. Hannah, typically, was silent. She didn't say much at these meetings, but she sure got the job done once it was determined. Arlette's lips were pressed together so tightly, her wrinkles looked like those stitches they put around scarecrows' mouths.

"Yes, Arlette?" Ida Mae asked, figuring they might as well get it out in the open, whatever it was.

"I just don't like the idea of going behind the bishop's back," she said, reaching into her bag and pulling out her knitting. "It feels sneaky."

Ida Mae bit back an exasperated sigh. "We're not going behind his back, Arlette. Let me ask you a question. You know how the Raleigh family has been down with the flu all week? Well, would it do any harm for one of us to make up a batch of soup and deliver it, without telling the bishop?"

"I guess not," Arlette said, concentrating on setting the heel of the sock she was working on, some monstrosity in chartreuse. Arlette did lovely work, but the colors she chose . . . New Year's Resolution. Right. Arlette did lovely work. Ida Mae left it at that.

"Well, that's all I'm saying." Ida Mae tried to make her tone soothing. "We can administrate in our capacity without having to alarm him over every sniffle in the ward. And, if something big comes up, we'll let him know."

"I suppose you're right. You are the president, after all, and so this is your stewardship." Arlette's tone sounded conciliatory, but Ida Mae waited for the other shoe to drop. And it did. "If this gets out of control, I know you'll handle it."

Ida Mae nodded. Leave it to Arlette to remind her of the trouble she'd be in if this didn't work. But it would work—and it wasn't like anything *bad* was going to happen. She pushed back the little voice that said, "But what if it does?" If it did, well, she wouldn't let it. That's all.

The remainder of the meeting was spent discussing the upcoming service project and visiting teaching. "I've asked Sister Bailey to join us at our next meeting," Ida Mae said. "She's been telling me of some holes in our visiting teaching assignments, and I thought if we all brainstormed, we could come up with a way to solve the problem."

"Next Tuesday at nine?" Hannah asked. Bless her; the meetings were every Tuesday at nine, but she never failed to ask and write it down.

"Yes, Hannah. Tuesday at nine."

The ladies were sent home after a mug of hot chocolate and two cookies apiece. The weather had been warm, but that morning Mother Nature realized it was still January and got back to work. Ida Mae wouldn't dream of sending anyone out in the cold without a warm stomach.

Rinsing out the last of the mugs, she let out the sigh she'd been holding in for the last hour. She wasn't given to pity parties, but every so often she had to wonder why she had been chosen for this calling. It was said, in their small Utah town of Omni, that if anything needed to be done, Ida Mae Babbitt was the one to ask. They even said she organized her first bake sale at the tender age of three weeks. She was sure that part wasn't true, but she did have a knack for running things.

She imagined it had something to do with the fact that her mother died in childbirth with her younger sister Lola, and Ida Mae was put in charge of the household. She knew how to plan something, get it done, and clean up afterward, but she excelled in doing it alone. She didn't know how to delegate. She didn't know how to trust someone else to follow through on their assignment, and to keep from becoming irritated when they didn't do it the way she would have. The Relief Society was about working together—it wasn't a one-woman show. She didn't know if she could learn to let go enough to be the kind of leader these women needed.

Chapter 2

"Aunt Ida Mae?" Ren stuck his head through the back door. "Oh, good. You're home."

"Where else would I be?" she asked. "You know I have meetings on Tuesday mornings. It would have to be a real emergency to drag me away."

"Well, sometimes things come up unexpectedly. Because, you know, they're *emergencies.*"

Ida Mae chose to ignore his flippant remark and concentrated instead on putting the mugs into the cupboard. Ren was her only nephew, the son of her sister, Lola. A bit of a free spirit, he sported an earring in his left ear—just a small one, but an earring nonetheless—and he hadn't decided what to be when he grew up. He didn't consider twenty-five to be grown up yet, obviously. He even had a small ponytail on the back of his head.

"So, I've dropped out of college," Ren said, taking a seat at the counter. He reached out and plucked a banana from the fruit bowl.

"Again?"

"No need to sound like I do it every day. This is only the third time."

"Three times is a bit more than usual, don't you think?" She handed him a napkin. "Don't people generally enroll and then, at some point down the road, graduate?"

"That's for people who want to live in a box." Ren half-rose and lobbed his banana peel into the garbage. "Three points."

"Two. Three would have been farther back, like, from the living room."

"Oh." He resumed his seat and rolled his napkin into a ball. "Listen, I don't know what's wrong with me. I tried to stick with it this time, I really did. But I was bored out of my mind. Why does society expect people to have college degrees? Why can't I just use what I know and get on with my life?"

Coming from anyone else, this would have sounded like a whiny, cheap excuse for avoiding an education. From Ren, though, it made perfect sense. The boy had been building his own mechanical gizmos since he could sit up, and had any number of inventions lining the shelves in his room. He could fix anything. He understood everything. From politics to lawnmowers to quantum physics, you could ask the boy anything and get an answer. It might not make sense, but it would be an answer nonetheless.

Ida Mae reached for the tea kettle, searching for something to do with her hands while she thought about Ren's question. He sat quietly, flicking his napkin back and forth on the counter.

"It all depends on what you want to do with your life," she said at last, watching the flame on the gas stove light with a spurt-spurt-spurt. "Do you want to work for a big corporation, or start one of your own? If you're the boss, it won't matter if you have a degree or not. Going to work for someone else might be another story."

"You know what I really want? I want to market my inventions. I've got a ton of 'em, and they're really useful, too. I could get patents, and then sell the rights, and make my living that way."

"Why don't you try it?" Ida Mae pulled the hot chocolate tin out of the cupboard. "You've still got the money from your mother's life insurance policy, don't you?"

"I haven't spent a dime of it," Ren said. "It felt weird, spending money that was only mine because my mother died."

"I know how you feel." Lola had also left a small bequest to Ida Mae, and it sat in the bank collecting interest. Lola's death had been sudden and shocking, an aneurism that burst the day after she turned fifty. She'd been too young to go, and Ren had been too young to understand. Ida Mae and her now deceased husband took Ren to live with them while he finished high school and dealt with his grief. She loved that boy like her own, and probably coddled him a good deal too much.

"What would it take to start?" she asked. "How do you get a patent, and how do you find someone interested in buying it?"

"I don't know, truthfully. I need to get on the Internet and see what I can find. Mind if I use yours? My roommate is studying for a big test, and I told him I'd scram so it would be nice and quiet."

"Sure, go ahead."

Ida Mae heard the sound of furious typing a few minutes later and allowed herself a smile. She would not be one bit surprised if the next Bill Gates himself was sitting in her spare bedroom, using her Dell. Ren could do anything he set his mind to. He just needed to set his mind to it longer than the fifteen minutes it took to learn more about it.

She pulled out the vacuum and was happily Hoovering when Ren emerged from the guest room, his hair somewhat pulled loose from his ponytail. "I found what I need to get started," he said when she turned the vacuum off and could hear him. "But listen, Aunt Ida Mae, there's another reason I'm here."

"What's that?" He had his I-don't-want-to-tell-you-this look, and she mentally braced herself.

"Well, since I'm not a student at the college anymore, and my apartment was in student housing, they want me to leave." He shifted from one foot to the other. "Any chance I could have my old room back for a while?"

Her heart gave a leap, an unaccustomed thing for it to do. She had missed that boy, no doubt about it. "Of course you can, Ren. I haven't done a thing with it. You can change that, though—the Spiderman bedspread is probably too young for you."

"I don't know," he said, leaning against the doorjamb and crossing his arms. "I haven't outgrown a lot of things I should have by now. But are you sure I won't be putting you out? I'll contribute to groceries and pay rent. I'm not going to freeload."

"You could never put me out, Ren," she protested. "Truth be told, it will do me good to have you around. It's been a little too lonely around here."

Something in her tone of voice must have betrayed her. Ren's eyebrows went up a notch. "Is everything okay, Aunt Ida Mae? You aren't going all melancholy on me, are you?"

"No, of course not. I don't have time for such nonsense." She began winding the cord on the vacuum. "It'll be good to have you back, that's all."

Ren crossed the room in four strides and wrapped his arms around her shoulders. "Thanks, Auntie. I really appreciate this."

"Are you sure you want to live clear out here, though? The closest big town is forty miles away."

"You've got a Walmart and a McDonald's, and that's good enough for me," he said. "I may head in to Salt Lake or Provo every so often to get parts, but I'm ready for some more country living."

"Have you got your things with you?"

"Just my overnight bag. I've still got another three days and figured I could clear out later."

"Bring it in and get settled, then. I'll start us a good old country lunch."

Ren grabbed his coat and went outside while Ida Mae rummaged through the fridge for the bottle of mustard that had somehow gotten shoved clear in the back. She couldn't help the smile that played around her lips. Ren was a little uncouth at times, and definitely unconventional. But she'd be "et for a tater" if she didn't love him like her own son.

Chapter 3

Jeannie Bailey accepted the napkin Ida Mae offered and wiped her plum-tinted lips. "Marvelous cookie, Ida Mae. I really shouldn't have, but I'm glad I did."

Ida Mae waved her hand. "It's nothing. Now, you were saying . . . ?"

"Oh, that's right. About visiting teaching." She pulled out her notebook. "We had sixty percent visiting teaching last month, which is up from November by eight percent. But we're still far from one hundred, and that's a fact."

Ida Mae nodded. She'd spoken at length to the sisters in Relief Society about the importance of keeping in touch with their assigned sisters, but out here not everyone had a phone, and there had been a lot of sickness over the winter. It was a shame so many sisters went unvisited every month.

"I do have one concern to mention, Ida Mae," Jeannie said. She leaned forward a little, the couch beneath her making the sound of doom. "Martha Anderson told me that when she went to visit the Dunn family this morning, she stepped into the kitchen to get a glass of water and noticed there wasn't any food in the cupboards. You know those glass cupboards they have? She could see the salt and pepper shakers, but nothing else."

Ida Mae frowned. True, they might have had food in the refrigerator, but experience had taught her that if there wasn't food in the cupboard, there often wasn't food anywhere in the house.

"Brother Dunn has been out of work for how long, now?" she asked.

"Four months," Hannah said, making one of her rare verbal contributions to the meeting.

"That's a long time. And they've never asked for help," Ida Mae mused. "I think it's time we did some investigating. I'll go over this afternoon."

"Wonderful." Jeannie beamed. "I knew you'd know what to do."

"We could take her over some fresh bread and jam," Tansy offered. "I did some baking this morning, and I have lots of strawberry jam from this summer."

"That would be nice," Ida Mae told her. "So, you'd like to go over with me?"

"I'd love to."

"I would, but I have a doctor's appointment," Arlette announced, flipping her knitting to start a new row. The socks from last week were a distant memory— this week's pair was cream. Something wasn't right. It wasn't like Arlette to use such a sedate color.

"That's all right, Arlette," Ida Mae told her. "Tansy and I will cover it."

After finalizing details on the visiting teaching assignments and talking about the upcoming blood drive, the sisters went home, and Ida Mae rubbed her temples. Mary Dunn was a sweet girl who probably couldn't be more than twenty-five and already had four children. Her husband, Nick, was a good-natured fellow who seemed to appreciate his gem of a wife and always spoke highly of her. She wished she had some sort of magic wand to wave and create a job for Nick, but in Omni, there just weren't a lot of businesses. Most of the families were supported by the turkey industry or they commuted into a larger town. It wasn't easy to live clear out here and still make a living.

That afternoon, bundled up to their chins, Tansy and Ida Mae picked their way up the icy walk to the Dunns' front door. Mary opened it, holding a baby on her hip. Ida Mae started to speak, but Tansy beat her to it.

"Mary? I made an extra loaf of bread this morning, and if you don't take it, I'll have to freeze it, and my Earl hates eating bread that's been frozen and then thawed. Would you please take it off my hands?"

Mary blinked, shifting the child to her other hip. "I suppose so . . ."

"Wonderful! We'll just bring it in for you. Your hands are full."

Tansy adeptly slipped into the house, leaving Ida Mae with a quirked eyebrow. Tansy was good. Really good.

Ida Mae followed her lead, and soon they were standing in the spotless kitchen.

"You can just set that on the table," Mary said, placing a pacifier in the child's mouth.

"Oh, but this is freezer jam," Tansy said. Before Mary could stop her, she opened the door, placing the container on the shelf. Ida Mae took a peek. The freezer was empty, with the exception of two ice cube trays.

Ida Mae pressed her lips together. "Mary, I think we should have a little talk," she said quietly, taking her by the elbow and guiding her into the living room.

Once seated, she came straight to the point. "You don't have food, do you?"

Mary looked down at the carpet. "We have a little. A bag of apples and some oatmeal."

"And when will you be able to get more?"

"Oh, Nick's bringing home some groceries tonight," she said. "He called and said he'd go shopping on the way home."

Ida Mae knew the girl was lying, but she didn't want to press her. "That's good. If you need anything, you let us know, okay? We can work wonders."

Mary smiled, although it looked stiff. "Okay, Sister Babbitt. I will."

Tansy held her tongue until they were back in Ida Mae's car, then she burst out, "Why isn't she telling us the truth?"

"I don't know." Ida Mae started the car and let it warm a minute, even though they'd only been inside a short time. "Maybe she's ashamed. Maybe she's feeling prideful. Maybe her husband doesn't want anyone to know he can't provide. I wish I knew." She pulled out onto the road, noting how deserted and lonely it was.

She took Tansy home and then pulled in her own driveway, mulling over the Dunns' situation. She'd been thinking the whole way home, but was no closer to an answer than when she started.

Ren was in the fridge making a sandwich out of leftover meatloaf. "Hi," he said, pulling out the mayonnaise. "Want one?"

"No, thanks," she said, trying to hide her shudder. There was nothing worse, in her opinion, than cold meatloaf. Unless it was cold meatloaf with mayonnaise, but trying to convince Ren to eat anything without mayonnaise was a hopeless proposition. The boy was positively addicted. "How was work?"

"Great." He had started work just that morning at the town's only VCR/DVD repair shop and movie rental store, Groovy Movies. "I fixed a jammed VCR and rented out all four copies of *The Phantom Menace*."

Ida Mae smiled. She'd never met such a Star Wars fanatic. "They were all rented on your recommendation, I assume."

"But of course." He took a huge bite of sandwich and chased it with a gulp of root beer. "How was your day?"

"Discouraging." She pulled out a chair and sat down, feeling older and heavier than she had in some time. "There's a family in our ward who's been unemployed for months, and I think they're out of food with no way to get more. She says they're going shopping tonight, but I just can't accept that. I wish I knew a way to tell if she was lying to me or not."

"Hmmm." Ren chewed thoughtfully, his face a study in concentration. "How opposed are you to a little spying?" he asked after several long moments.

"Spying?" Ida Mae's head came up. "What on earth do you mean?"

"Well, what if I came up with a way for you to tell if she was lying?"

She shook her head. "As tempting as that is, Ren, it's her responsibility. Even if I catch her in a lie, it's her choice to lie to me, and her choice not to ask for help."

"You said this was a family. Are there children, then?"

Ida Mae saw the Dunns' four children in her mind, two girls and two boys, ranging in age from six to one year. They were darling little things, and the thought of them going hungry . . . "What do you have in mind?" she asked.

"I have this gizmo that's no bigger than a cockroach, but it's a camera," he said. "You stick it somewhere, and it can see everything in the room. The only problem is, you have to be within a thousand yards of it to pick up the picture on the receiver. I guess you could say, it's a *bug* I haven't worked out."

She chose to ignore the pun. "What are you thinking?"

"What if you placed this camera somewhere in the kitchen? Then you could see what food goes in and comes out. You'd know if she was lying or not, and you'd know if they needed you to bring them food."

Ida Mae shook her head. "I just don't know, Ren. That sounds . . . illegal."

He shrugged. "It was just a thought."

She pushed herself up and walked over to the fridge. She couldn't deny the light she'd seen in Ren's eyes when he talked about his camera. This was his life's dream, and if his invention really worked, he could be set. And those hungry children . . . her eyes fell on the kitchen magnet her visiting teachers had brought over. It was a dried flower encased in plastic, and attached was a card. "If you need anything, give us a call," it stated in cheery handwriting, complete with names and telephone numbers. Her brain began to churn.

"I think I have a way to get that camera into the house," she told Ren. "I need to call an emergency meeting."

○—

"It's a wonderful idea!" Tansy clasped her hands together, reminding Ida Mae of a sixty-year-old Cupie Doll. "We can't let those poor children go hungry, now, can we?"

"I don't like it. I don't like it at all," Arlette said. "You'd be breaking—how many laws?" She clacked her needles together for emphasis. "The last thing Bishop Sylvester needs is for his entire Relief Society presidency to end up serving jail time."

"It's more exciting than serving funeral potatoes," Tansy shot back.

"Hey, now, let's not be harsh," Ren pled. "I have enjoyed many a pan of funeral potatoes in my time, and I don't think they deserve to be spoken of in such a fashion."

Ida Mae held up her hands. "Let's all think about this rationally, shall we? On one hand, we would be breaking some laws. Well, only one, that I can think of—we wouldn't be trespassing, really—we'd just be spying. I suppose it is a little nosy, and we are interfering with free agency. If it was just Mary and Nick, I'd say, leave them to their own decisions. But we've got young children involved, and if they were to exercise *their* agency, I'm sure they would choose to eat rather than not. Are we agreed on that much, at least?" All around the room, heads nodded.

"Couldn't you just . . . leave the food anyway?" Hannah spoke up, bouncing Baby Jeremiah on her hip. Her other son, Joey, played quietly in the corner with his cars.

"Let's not get hasty!" Ren jumped into the conversation again, forgetting his role as advisor and inventor only. "I'd really like the chance to try my toy out in real life. If it works, I can sell it for a heap."

"To whom? Thugs? Miscreants?" Arlette shook a magenta sock at him. "I don't know what you're up to, young man, but I'd be worried about you if I were Ida Mae."

"Well, you're not," Ida Mae reminded her. "And we're getting off track. I don't want to strain our allotted resources by taking food to people who don't need it. If Nick does come home with groceries tonight, then we'll have all that food to give someone else. And if he doesn't, then we'll know what to do."

Arlette pressed her lips together. Ida Mae watched her out of the corner of her eye. Budgeting was Arlette's specialty, and Ida Mae knew she was calculating the cost of wasted food.

"Very well, then," she said. "But I'd better go along to make sure you only break *one* law."

"This is so exciting!" Tansy gave a little bounce in her seat. Ida Mae cringed. How long would the springs hold up under that kind of strain?

"I wish I could go," Hannah said. "But Jeremiah will need his nap."

"We'll fill you in on all the details," Ida Mae promised. "Now, let's make our plans."

Chapter 4

Tansy and Ida Mae retraced their steps to the Dunns' front door, avoiding all the ice patches. Mary answered with a different child on her hip, but the same tired expression on her face.

"Sisters! I didn't expect to see you again," she said. Ida Mae couldn't decide if her expression was one of surprise or dismay.

"I got all the way home and remembered I forgot something," Tansy said. Coming from anyone else, a sentence like that would have been laughable, but from Tansy, it fit.

She rummaged in her bag and brought out a card, decorated with a huge silk flower. "This is a fridge magnet," she said, handing it to Mary. "It has all our phone numbers on it. You just go ahead and hang it right on your fridge, and then if you need anything, you just call us. In the meantime, it will hold your shopping lists or coupons or anything else. It really is very strong."

Mary turned the card and read the words on the front. "Thank you," she said, moving it out of the grasp of the child on her hip. "I'll hang it up right now."

She closed the door after the sisters stepped off the porch. Ida Mae shook her head as she pulled out her keys. "You're a wonder, Tansy. I bet you could infiltrate the Mafia, and they'd never know what hit them."

"I've never tried," Tansy replied artlessly. "Do they need it?"

Ren and Arlette looked up from their seats in the back of the car as Ida Mae and Tansy climbed in.

"Slick as a whistle," Ida Mae said. "We've got our own Miss Marple here."

"Well, I wouldn't say that," Tansy said, glowing with modest pride. "I just did what had to be done."

"Okay, step two," Ren said. "I've established a connection, and I can see the inside of the house now. The magnet has been placed on the fridge, and I count no fewer than twelve fingers trying to grab it. No— make that fifteen. There was a petal in the way and I couldn't count right."

"Sorry," Ida Mae said. "I tried to glue the flower so the whole lens would be free, but then the lens was too visible."

"It's okay. I can see enough. She just scooted the magnet up higher, thank goodness. I wasn't in the mood to get an insider's view of a child's mouth. You know how they taste everything." Ren adjusted the settings on his laptop. "Okay, you can go."

Ida Mae drove a short distance down the road and parked in a small stand of trees. Everyone fell silent as they waited.

Ida Mae glanced over her shoulder, noting the look of satisfaction on Ren's face. He was in his element. She wondered, not for the first time, if she had agreed to this crazy scheme for Ren's benefit and not just for the Dunns'.

"Why couldn't we just stake out their house from the front?" Arlette wanted to know. "We'd be able to see if Nick brought sacks or not."

"There aren't any trees or other houses across from them. We'd be completely obvious," Ida Mae said.

"So, let me get this straight. In order to help preserve someone else's pride, we're making ourselves look like fools?"

Tansy turned and looked at Arlette with a beaming smile. "That's right! Isn't this fun?"

"So what happens when the camera's battery runs down?" Arlette asked. "It certainly can't last very long."

"That's the beauty of the whole fridge-magnet thing," Ren said. "It doesn't even need batteries. I added a teeny little gyro-generator to the back of the card that's kept spinning by the magnet. It'll power the camera almost forever."

The sun was nearly down, and they had exhausted the hot cocoa in Ida Mae's thermos when Nick's car passed them on the road. "That's him," Ida Mae said, excitement making her voice catch in her throat. "Are you ready, Ren?"

"Everything's still working fine," he said. "I've got a shot of the kitchen door and table."

Arlette muttered something under her breath.

"What was that?" Ida Mae asked.

"I was just wondering what color our prison uniforms are going to be," she said. "I look terrible in orange."

"I look good in peach," Tansy said. "I was told that I'm a spring."

"A spring what? Certainly not a spring chicken," Arlette retorted.

Ida Mae sighed. She didn't know if this was good-natured bantering or contention. With Arlette, one didn't know a lot of things.

"Show time!" Ren exclaimed. Arlette leaned over and peered at the screen with him.

"Nick is coming in. His arms are empty."

A gust of disappointment escaped Ida Mae's lips.

"But he's taking something out of his pocket. It's money! He just set it on the table."

"That's good! He must have just gotten a job," Tansy said.

"But Mary doesn't look happy," Ren said. "She's yelling something."

"Doesn't this thing have a microphone?" Arlette asked.

"Nope, 'fraid not." Ren paused, then whistled. "She just picked up the money and threw it at him. It's fluttering all over the place. Wow—there must be over a thousand dollars."

"If he just got a job today, how would he get a thousand dollars?" Ida Mae asked. "Mary would have told us if he'd been hired somewhere, and jobs don't often pay you the first day out. There's usually a two-week or more wait, I thought."

"Maybe there was a signing bonus." Ren pushed a few more buttons. "Well, they've left the kitchen. I think they're going to be okay—that money will get them the groceries they need."

Ida Mae started the car. "Well, I'm glad to hear that," she said, pulling back onto the road. "I don't like to think of those children without any milk."

"Many children do just fine without milk," Arlette said. "We never had it—we were lactose intolerant."

"What did you do for calcium?" Tansy asked.

"Broccoli," Arlette replied. She was quiet for a minute, then added, "I can't eat a stalk of broccoli to this day. And thank goodness for the discovery of soy milk."

Ida Mae dropped everyone off, then she and Ren returned to their house. "Your little toy was a success," she said as she rinsed out her thermos. "Why don't you look happy about it?"

"It just occurred to me, I don't have a way to get it back," he said. "It's pretty much stuck there on the Dunns' fridge."

"Did you keep a list of parts? Can you make another one?"

"Oh, sure, that's not a problem. It's just that I really was sort of attached to that one."

"I didn't realize you could get attached to little . . . tiny camera things," Ida Mae said lamely, not knowing what to call the gizmo Ren invented.

"I get attached to everything," he said, walking toward his room. "That's the problem."

Ida Mae watched him close the door, wondering what he meant. She imagined he'd tell her in time— he was never able to keep a secret for long, especially from her.

She opened the fridge and pulled out the eggs, deciding to mix up a batch of muffins for the next morning's breakfast. As she stirred, she counted up all her sins and their consequences. She'd be released from her calling. She'd go to jail. She'd take her entire presidency with her. Bishop Sylvester would be very disappointed.

She finished the batter and put the muffin tin in the oven. Everyone would wonder what on earth had happened to her. Her children would be ashamed.

At that, she started to laugh. Her children hardly ever thought of her as it was. Neither of them had been to see her in a couple of years—maybe it would be good for them to worry about her for a while, instead of the other way around.

Chapter 5

"Aunt Ida Mae?"

Ida Mae put down her feather duster and walked toward the sound of Ren's voice. She found him in the garage, taking some of his equipment out of his car and placing it on a shelf.

"What is it?" she asked when she saw the look of concern on his face.

"Well, you know the Dunns?" he asked, as if she hadn't had them on her mind every minute of every day—well, practically—since the starving baby scare the week before.

"Yes?" she said patiently, reminding herself of her New Year's Resolution. How long did a body have to keep one of those things, anyway?

"Can we talk?"

She nearly asked him if he was doing a Joan Rivers impersonation, but she could tell he was serious and in no mood for her rare show of levity. She squelched it as quickly as it had come up, and they went into the kitchen, Ren with his laptop under his arm.

"I was delivering a DVD player to the old Palmer place, you know, that shack clear out there," he said, waving his hand in the wrong direction, but Ida Mae knew where he meant and didn't correct him. "Well, there are two ways to get there, and I drove past the Dunns' on the way back. My laptop was on because I was working on a spreadsheet."

This she could not ignore. "You were typing and driving at the same time?"

"I was driving slowly, and there was no one around for miles," Ren protested. "It was perfectly safe."

She clamped her mouth down. Hard. She winced.

"Anyway, as I was driving past, I picked up a transmission from the camera on the Dunns' fridge. I was going to ignore it, but then I decided to record it instead." He turned the laptop toward her. "I need to show you something."

"Oh, Ren, I don't want to spy on those poor people anymore," Ida Mae protested. "I've got my temple recommend interview coming up in two months, and I've already got enough repenting to do as it is."

"But you've got to see this," he said. He reached out and pushed the play button. Unable to contain her curiosity, Ida Mae watched.

Nick Dunn was talking to a large man in a black leather jacket. "Isn't that a sweet jacket?" Ren said. "I've always wanted one of those."

"Hush," Ida Mae said, even though the clip had no sound.

Nick waved his hands, looking upset. The man in black reached inside his jacket, took out an envelope, and handed it to Nick. Nick shook his head, but the man waved a finger in his face and set the envelope on the table. He left, and Nick sank into his chair, putting his head in his hands. The clip ended.

"What happened after that?" Ida Mae asked.

"It was time to make dinner. The wife came in and started to chop celery."

"Hmm." Ida Mae rested her elbows on the table. "We have no idea what's in that envelope, but whatever it was, Nick was sure upset by it."

"I think it was more money," Ren said. "It looked just like the envelopes of money they use in mobster movies."

"So, all mobsters shop at the same office supply store?" Ida Mae asked.

"Sure. I bet they get a group discount." Ren grinned, then closed the lid of his laptop. "What are we going to do, Aunt Ida Mae?"

"What do you think we should do? All we know is that the boy was given an envelope he didn't want. Maybe it was a bill from his dentist. Or a letter from an ex-girlfriend. You can't go leaping to conclusions, Ren. I think we've had ourselves a bit of excitement, and now we're craving more. The fact is, we did our job, and the children have food. That's all we set out to accomplish. End of story."

Ida Mae's words sounded firm in her own ears, yet as she put dinner on the table, she couldn't help but wonder. Just what was going on at the Dunns' house that had Nick so upset? He was usually pretty laid back.

The phone rang, interrupting her thoughts. In her "pre-Relief-Society-president" life, she would have let the machine get it. After all, that's why they invented the answering machine, right? But ever since she was set apart, she felt a pull toward the phone when it rang. Funny, she didn't remember that being part of the blessing.

She set the mashed potatoes down and reached for the cordless—another marvelous invention, obviously designed by a busy mother. Who else would have so desperately needed the ability to wander around the house and talk at the same time?

The Caller ID—another necessary addition to her already-high phone bill—read "Hunter, Reed." She pushed "talk" immediately.

"Hello, Sister Babbitt?" Reed Hunter's usually tremulous voice sounded even more shaky over the phone.

"What can I do for you, Brother Hunter?"

"It's Mother. She's had another fall, and they're afraid she may have broken her hip."

Ida Mae closed her eyes. She'd been around enough broken hips to know that when an elderly person took a spill of that magnitude, it usually meant their time was near.

"What would you like me to do?"

"Could you come see her at the hospital? She's always liked you. She says you have a way of setting the record straight."

Ida Mae bit back a sardonic chuckle. "I'll be down. What room is she in?"

"They don't have her in a room yet—she's still in x-ray. But I thought I'd better give you a call right away, you know, in case . . ."

Ida Mae mentally finished his unspoken thought. "I understand."

"And we don't know yet if they'll be keeping her here or taking her in to Salt Lake. So, I guess I should call you and let you know . . . I'm sorry. I should have found that out before calling. I just couldn't think of what else to do."

"It's all right, Brother Hunter. You let me know where she is, and I'll be there."

"Thank you." His relief fairly dripped through the phone.

Ida Mae grabbed her pen and made a notation on the calendar. "What about you and Heidi? Do you need anything?"

"Heidi is a bit shaken up—she and Mother had a bit of a set-to last night, and she's blaming herself for Mother's accident, even though it happened twelve hours later. I keep telling her that she didn't plan for Mother to trip on a slipper, but she's taking it hard all the same."

Ida Mae made another note: *chocolate*. There was nothing like a hunk of the brown stuff to soothe the savage beast, or in this case, the upset pre-menopausal woman.

"I'll do what I can, Brother Hunter," she promised, hanging up and turning back to her dinner table. She had some chocolate chip cookie dough in the freezer—she'd take it out and bake it first thing in the morning. With any luck, the cookies would still be warm by the time she made the delivery. She tapped a finger on her lips. Something was missing— salad dressing. She turned and grabbed a bottle each of Ranch and Catalina and placed them next to the green salad.

"Ren, dinner's ready."

Ren came a moment later, his hair still wet from the quick shower he had taken while she pulled the meal together. "Smells wonderful, as always," he said, nodding appreciatively at the arrangement of food. "You sure have a way with a table."

"I see no point in eating ugly food," Ida Mae said. "It may all taste the same if you close your eyes, but if you can make it pretty, why not?"

"Why not, indeed?" Ren speared a radish rose with his fork. "I thought you didn't like radishes."

"I don't. But they add a little color to the salad, so I suffer in silence."

The meal proceeded in silence, too—the only sound was the click of knife and fork against the plate. "Manna from heaven," Ren pronounced, scooting his chair back at long last. "If I keep eating like that, I'm going to gain a hundred pounds."

"I do light meals as well," she told him. "How do you suppose I keep my girlish figure?"

He smiled, but the expression faded. "Aunt Ida Mae, have you thought any more about what I told you?"

"You mean about the Dunns?" She had to confess, between getting dinner on and the call from Brother Hunter, she hadn't given it another thought.

"Yes. I really think there's something going on there."

"I have to run in to the hospital tomorrow. While I'm out, I'll swing by and see how Mary's doing, all right? If she seems upset at all, we'll know we need to look into things."

Ren nodded. "I guess that will work."

"What's the alternative? Setting up camp in a tent and monitoring their every move?"

"Hey, that sounds like fun!"

She held up a hand. "I was joking. Ren, I love mystery novels as much as you do. But this is Omni. Nothing ever happens here. We have no crime element. We have no drug dealers. We don't even speed. It's just not likely that something suspicious is going on."

"You're probably right." He stood and gathered her plate along with his. "I'm on dishes tonight."

She blinked. When was the last time someone else had done dishes in her house? Probably four years.

But only because I didn't accept offers of help, she realized belatedly. She really was going to have to loosen up.

○━

Ida Mae drove her car into the insufficient Omni Hospital parking lot and found a space not too terribly far from the door. She checked with the nurse, then stuck her head into the elderly Sister Hunter's room. The lady was alone and appeared to be asleep, but as Ida Mae stepped back to leave, she heard,

"I smell cookies."

"Yes, you do, Rose." Ida Mae stepped over the threshold and approached the bed, her paper plate held in front of her like a ring bearer's pillow. "Fresh baked this morning."

"You are a lifesaver." Rose Hunter raised her head and looked at Ida Mae. "How did you know I needed a good cookie today?"

"I didn't need a crystal ball to see that one." Ida Mae took the foil off one edge of the plate and pulled out a cookie, placing it in Rose's hand.

"I wish I could sit up," Rose said. "I'm going to get crumbs in my bed."

"No, you won't," Ida Mae told her. "You'll eat 'em all and none of them will end up in your bed."

She took a seat while Rose ate, then helped her reach the water.

"Absolutely delicious," Rose said, resting her head against her pillow once more. "You know how to cheer a person up."

"I took a plate over to Heidi before I came here," Ida Mae said. "That poor girl is just beside herself."

"I wish she wouldn't take it so hard. Sure, we had a little fight, but it's one I've wanted to have for years. It sure made me feel better—I don't know why she's hanging on to it like this."

"You wanted to fight?"

"Well, you know how it is. There's stuff that has to be cleared out of the air, and once it's gone, you like each other better for it."

Ida Mae nodded. She'd had that experience herself, many times.

"Heidi's been a good daughter-in-law. I have nothing to fault her for." Rose reached for her water, missed by a mile, and Ida Mae helped bring it to her lips.

"Tell her for me, will you?" Rose wiped the corner of her mouth with the tissue balled up in her hand. "Tell her I don't blame her for this at all. She won't listen to me."

"I will. Now, tell me about your hip. When Reed called this morning, he said it wasn't broken."

"They think it's just bruised, thank goodness. I've got a whole lot of living left to do before my days are over."

Rose Hunter was a tough old bird, Ida Mae thought affectionately. Nearly as ornery as Ida Mae herself, Rose held her own in any argument or discussion. It was only two years ago, at the age of eighty, that she came to live with Reed and Heidi. A broken ankle had been the culprit that time, and when it healed, everyone decided it was best if she just stayed on. She loved her independence and came kicking and screaming, but she told Ida Mae later that she didn't know what she would have done if Reed and Heidi hadn't taken her in.

"Do you ever think about your husband?"

The question was asked softly, but it slapped Ida Mae upside the head. She blinked and fought back a rush of emotion before answering,

"Of course I do. He's been dead for six years, but I think about him every day."

"My Evan has been gone for seventeen. He was killed in a farming accident when we lived in Santaquin. My children were raised, of course, so there was just me to worry about, and I've done fine. But lately, I've really been missing him."

Ida Mae would not think about Henry. She would not do it. She leaned forward and concentrated on Rose's relaxed face. The woman was drifting off to sleep, sharing her memories as she went.

"We were married when I was sixteen. My father came right up out of his chair when I told him I was engaged—he went looking for his shotgun. I told him there was no need. Evan and I were in love, and we were going to build a home together. My father decided that being married was its own punishment, and let us go through with it. Evan was nineteen, but already established with a little farm of his own."

Her voice got softer the more she talked, and soon she was breathing the deep rhythm of the asleep. Ida Mae sat for a few more minutes, then rose slowly and slipped out of the room. She had too much to do to dwell on her own past; she'd much rather help others deal with theirs.

Chapter 6

"Thank you for coming, sisters," Ida Mae said, bringing the meeting to order. "I don't think we have any old business, do we?"

Hannah shook her head.

"All right, then, let's see what's on the agenda for this week."

Tansy bounced nervously in her chair.

"Yes, Tansy?"

"Well, I wasn't supposed to say anything. Ren made me promise, but I just can't hold it in."

"What does Ren have to do with the workings of the Relief Society?" Ida Mae was exasperated. That foolish boy wasn't still going on about the Dunns, was he? She'd been to the house as promised and found Mary in good spirits. The children seemed happy. The house was warm. What more was there to say or do?

"Well, more than he'd like," Tansy said. "Is he here? He promised he'd help me explain."

Ida Mae pulled in a long, deep breath. Tansy felt she needed backup? What on earth . . .

"Ren?" she called out. "Your accomplice needs you."

Ren appeared immediately, giving credence to Ida Mae's suspicion that he'd been lurking in the hallway.

"Just what have you and Tansy been up to?"

"It's like this," Tansy said, even though she'd clearly indicated she wanted Ren to do the talking. "I called here the other day, and you were out. My car wouldn't start, and I needed a ride to the store. Ren came and got me, and we had a great time. I found a sale on Lofthouse sugar cookies, and I remembered Mary saying one time that her children really liked that brand. I thought we'd take a box out to them."

"You wanted to spy," Ida Mae interjected, and Arlette clicked her tongue.

"Okay, so I wanted to spy. That family's situation hasn't been sitting right with me for days now. And Ren came too, so I figured there really wasn't any harm in it."

"Ren is not your passport to freedom, Tansy," Ida Mae remonstrated. "I'd say he's your ticket to trouble."

"Aunt Ida Mae, I'm not as bad as all that," Ren piped up. "Let her finish."

Ida Mae crossed her arms and fixed Tansy with what she thought was a piercing glare. Tansy was unfazed as she proceeded with her tale.

"We took the cookies in, and the children were so happy to get them. Mary invited us to sit and have a cookie ourselves, along with some milk. And that's . . . when Ren did it."

"Did what?" A tremor of premonition raced through Ida Mae's veins. *Oh, say he didn't. Please do not say he did what I'm afraid he did.*

"He placed a bug in the living room."

Ida Mae exhaled, her worst fears coming true. "Ren, I cannot believe you did that. Another law broken, another thing I'm going to have to confess—what are you trying to do?"

"Why did you take a bug to the Dunns'?" Arlette looked confused. "And what kind was it?"

"A bug is a listening device," Ren explained.

"I just don't believe it." Arlette's knitting needles flew furiously, orange yarn slithering through her fingers like worms on steroids. "Ida Mae, of all the things . . ."

"Believe me, I know. Ren, Tansy, how could you do such a thing?"

"It's like this, Auntie." Ren leaned forward, putting his gangly elbows on his equally gangly knees.

"I watched that clip over and over, and I couldn't tell for sure if Nick was happy or mad. I could tell he was excited, but that was all, and I thought, you can be excited because you're happy *or* because you're mad. I just wanted an answer."

"I will take responsibility for placing the camera," Ida Mae said, shaking her finger at him, "but you didn't place that bug under the auspices of the Relief Society. I will not protect you if that comes to light." She said this firmly, knowing full well she'd bail him out if she had to.

"We need to tell the bishop about this," Arlette proclaimed, and Ida Mae nodded. Things had gone way too far. They needed to pull out while they could. But Tansy spoke up.

"But we can't! I was over to see Sister Sylvester just last night. She's still on bed rest, and her sister has come to live and take care of things. The poor bishop's blood pressure has only gone down two points, and the medication they put him on isn't helping. Please, let's not, Ida Mae. Please."

Ida Mae rolled her eyes at the ceiling. It was one thing to take care of a few problems without the bishop's knowledge, but it was quite another to listen to someone else's private conversations.

"This is what we will do," Ida Mae spoke after

pausing for several seconds. "We'll go back, we'll come up with a reason to go into the house, and we'll remove the bug. We'll tell Mary that I wrote one of the phone numbers wrong on the card we gave her, and I will take back the camera, replacing it with a different card. We are going to pull ourselves out of this as swiftly and as deftly as we can, and then we are never, ever, going to do anything like this again."

Tansy looked like she might cry. Ren's head was hung down—the boy really reminded her of a basset hound. Hannah's eyes were wide. Arlette was the only person in the room who looked as though she agreed with Ida Mae. Be that as it may, the proclamation had been made.

"When do we go?" Arlette said.

"This very afternoon."

They agreed to meet at Arlette's at one o'clock and ride out together. Ida Mae didn't know why that arrangement was made—surely she and Tansy alone could handle it, but Ren wouldn't be left out for anything, and Arlette was determined to oversee the retrieval and make sure justice was served.

"I wish I could go," Hannah mourned, and Ida Mae patted her shoulder.

"It's okay, dear. The next time we do something illegal, we'll hire you a sitter, and you can come along."

The girl brightened, and Ida Mae stifled a sigh. She was trying to be facetious, but Hannah had taken her seriously. Were they all so starved for something to do that espionage seemed like a fun afternoon activity?

○—

Ren drove, on Arlette's insistence, and the minivan pulled up in a clearing not far from the Dunns' house.

"We'll walk from here," Ida Mae explained. "If Mary looked out the window and saw all of you sitting out here, we'd have a hard time explaining ourselves."

"Do you have the new card?" Arlette asked.

"Right here," Tansy said, patting her oversized shoulder bag.

Ida Mae reached out to open her door, but the cackling sound of a speaker interrupted her movement.

"It's just not right." Mary Dunn's voice filled the van. "You can't do it any more."

"It's not that big of a deal," Nick said. "Really, it's not."

"I don't like it, Nick. I don't like it at all."

The voices moved away from the bug, and the people in the van weren't able to hear anything else. Then a children's television show began to play, and Ren clicked his laptop off.

"Well, what do you make of that?" Ida Mae asked.

"Something is definitely not right in that house," Arlette proclaimed.

"I knew we were dealing with something fishy," Ren added.

Tansy, for once in her life, was silent.

Ida Mae tapped her lips with her finger, thinking. What had they just overheard? Mary was obviously displeased with Nick's new line of work. She said *it just wasn't right.* That meant morally wrong, didn't it, and that generally meant illegal.

"It's time to go see the sheriff," she said after thinking it over.

O—

Sheriff Ricky Shelton leaned forward and put his massive elbows on his desk. "Let me get this straight, Ida Mae. You overheard Mary Dunn tell her husband . . ." he checked his notes. "That it wasn't right and she didn't like it."

"That's right." By tacit agreement, the ladies had decided not to tell the sheriff about the bug and the camera unless they absolutely had to.

"And Nick came home with money last week."

"Correct."

Ricky leaned back and let out a gust of air that fluffed his bangs. "Ida Mae, I don't know what to tell you. Nick's been looking for work and has apparently found a way to earn money. I should think you'd be happy for him."

Ida Mae bristled. "Of course I'm happy for him. I just wonder—"

"Furthermore," Ricky continued over Ida Mae's response, "Mary could have meant anything by what she said. My wife gets on me all the time for playing too many computer games. She tells me I should stop and that I'm neglecting her and the kids. If someone were to overhear us, you might think I was having an affair, from the arguments we have. But when you know the whole story, there's nothing sinister going on at all."

"But, Sheriff—"

"Ida Mae, I think you ladies should go home and tend to whatever Relief Society business is waiting for you and just stop worrying about this. I would need a whole lot more evidence of wrong doing before I could even start an investigation. If you happen to find some, let me know." He turned to Ren. "Keep an eye on these ladies, all right?"

"That was so disheartening," Tansy said as they climbed back into the van. "I thought the law was there to serve and protect."

"You have to admit, we didn't have a lot to tell him," Arlette pointed out. "I imagine we sounded pretty foolish."

"But that's what we brought Ren for. To give us an air of credibility." Tansy stuck her finger at the young man in question. "And he didn't even say anything!"

"What do you think, Ida Mae?" Arlette asked.

Ida Mae clicked her seat belt while she contemplated her answer. "There's something going on in that house," she said at last. "I'm sure of it."

"And it's not computer games," Tansy interjected. "About three months ago, Mary wanted to track a package online and asked if she could use my computer to do it, since they don't have one."

"The sheriff didn't mean computer games specifically," Arlette said. "He just meant there are any number of reasons why Mary could be upset with Nick right now."

"If I know anything about women, they're upset most of the time," Ren said, breaking the silence that had descended upon him as they had entered the police station. Ida Mae looked at him sharply. There was a story linked to that statement; she was sure of it. She'd have to squeeze it out of him later.

"Well, Ida Mae? What should we do?"

Arlette's question gave Ida Mae the opening to say what she'd been contemplating for the last five minutes. "I think we should keep investigating and come up with some of this evidence the sheriff asked for."

"He did give us permission to keep digging, in a round-about sort of way," Tansy said.

"Yes, he did. And we've done our civic duty—we went to the police, just as we should, and we were told to keep looking. That makes it our job to keep looking." Ida Mae hoped she wasn't justifying their actions too much, but someone had to look into the situation, and this was the only way she could come up with. If the sheriff didn't believe her, she doubted the bishop would, if she told him, which she wasn't going to.

"What should we call ourselves?" Tansy asked a moment later as they turned onto Arlette's road.

"What do you mean?" Ida Mae asked.

"Well, we should have a name for our organization. How about . . ." Tansy hummed thoughtfully for a moment. "The Relief Society Secret Service!"

"No, we can't use that," Arlette said.

"Why not?"

"The Relief Society is an organization of the Church. If we used it as part of our name, I'm sure there would be some copyright issues somewhere."

Ida Mae sighed inwardly, struggling to make her voice gentle. "But the Church, hopefully, will never know. That's why we're doing this in secret." She didn't see the need to name their covert operation, but Tansy seemed so thrilled by it, she would go along.

"But Arlette does have a point. What if someone wrote a book about us? *They* could get in trouble." Tansy thought another minute, not seeing Ida Mae's eyes roll. "How about Secret Sisters?"

"Much better," Arlette said, and Ida Mae nodded. Now that small issue was resolved, they could concentrate on more important things.

"What should we do first?" Tansy asked.

"We need to get some surveillance going," Ren said. "I don't work today at all. Why don't I take the first shift. Aunt Ida Mae, you come along with me. Tansy and Arlette, you can watch tomorrow night. I'll show you how to work all my gizmos."

"Why are we only watching at night?" Tansy asked.

"Most evil takes place at night," Arlette informed her. "Evil loves darkness."

Tansy shook her head. "It was daylight when Nick brought home the money."

"And when the man came to deliver that envelope," Arlette said.

Ida Mae pursed her lips. Tansy and Arlette made good points. But they couldn't bring anyone else in to help them—they were taking enough risks as they were, and it would be best if the entire 2nd ward didn't end up in jail. Who would staff the nursery?

"We'll take random shifts," she said at last. "We'll just hope something incriminating happens while we're watching."

"I wish my camera had a longer range," Ren said, sounding rueful. "It would be so nice if we could just kick back at home and keep an eye on things."

"I'm sure your next model will be much more powerful," Tansy consoled him, and he perked up at the thought.

They pulled into Arlette's driveway and separated to get into their individual vehicles. "Let us know what happens tonight," Tansy called out, and Ren raised a hand in acknowledgement.

"I honestly don't know what we're getting ourselves into," Ida Mae confessed as the engine in Ren's car sprang to life. "One minute I'm coordinating visiting teaching, and the next, I'm jail bait."

Ren started to laugh. "You're jail bait, are you?"

"Well, aren't I?"

"Um, not exactly. I'll explain later."

He directed the car into the Walmart parking lot. "I think we need to stock up on snacks," he said. "What should we get for our stakeout?"

"On TV, they always have coffee and donuts," Ida Mae said. "We could do hot chocolate and donuts, or a nice herbal tea, to keep us warm."

They ended up with a dozen donuts—half of them filled, for Ren—a bag of Doritos and a six-pack of A&W root beer. Ida Mae insisted on some baby carrots, although she was sure neither of them would open the package.

They put their loot in the trunk of the car, preparatory for that night's high jinks, and went about the rest of their day as if they weren't planning something nefarious. Ida Mae visited a few ladies on her list, arranged for meals to be brought in to a sick woman and her three children, and made a call for the upcoming service project. Ren sent some e-mails, took a nap, and played Tetris for an hour. All in all, it was a productive day.

"I just got off the phone with Missy Hopkins," Ida Mae said. "She'll tend Hannah's kids so she can come with us."

"You were serious about getting her a sitter?" Ren's voice sounded incredulous.

"I wasn't serious when I made the promise, because I thought this would all be over," Ida Mae explained. "But a promise is a promise."

Next came the task of deciding what to wear. Ren was of the opinion that they should wear brown capes, like Jedi knights, but neither of them owned a cape, let alone a brown one. Then he suggested they wear camouflage, but they encountered the same problem. Ida Mae thought they should dress warmly, and that's what they settled on.

Two hours later, their snacks secreted in the trunk and Hannah sitting in the back seat, they parked in "their" clearing, and Ren set up the equipment. Ida Mae had to admit, even though she was opposed to everything they were doing, it did carry a certain amount of excitement—possibly even better than making funeral potatoes.

They sat still at first, afraid they might miss something, but the Dunns' house was fairly quiet, just the normal noises of putting children to bed and cleaning up after supper. When they realized Nick wasn't even home yet, they started talking amongst themselves. Ida Mae was surprised to find out just how talkative Hannah could be, given half a chance.

"And have you found anyone to take your basement apartment?"

Hannah shook her head. "It's just a one bedroom and has a tiny kitchen, so we've been having a hard time getting it filled."

Ida Mae nodded. Even if a young couple took it, soon they'd start a family and have to move. There didn't seem to be such a thing as permanence any more. She'd been in the same house for thirty years, but these days, that seemed impossible.

Silence fell in the car again. After several long moments, Ren said, "I've got some CDs in that case by your feet, Auntie. Why don't you pick something out?"

Ida Mae zipped the case open and flipped through Ren's collection. "You like Tom Jones?" she asked.

"Why are you surprised? It's not unusual."

"Well, I was in the mood for some Glenn Miller."

They compromised with Harry Connick Jr., and listened until Nick's car passed them and turned into the drive.

"Here we go," Ren said.

Nick's voice filled the speaker. "Hi, honey."

"Hi," Mary replied. "I saved you some tofu meatloaf."

"Tofu?" Ida Mae interjected. "I knew the girl was health conscious, but gracious! Whoever heard of a tofu meatloaf?"

"Thanks," Nick said.

Neither Nick nor Mary said one more word to each other the rest of the evening.

"Now, that's not normal," Ida Mae said as they decided to wrap things up. "What couple goes an entire night without talking to each other?"

"Sometimes I don't talk to my husband," Hannah said.

Ida Mae pressed her lips together to keep herself from saying something sarcastic. She could believe Hannah would go for long periods of time without talking to her husband—she hardly spoke as it was.

"Why?" Ren asked, which, Ida Mae had to admit, was a pretty good question.

"Sometimes I'm upset with him, and sometimes I'm mad at someone else, and I don't want to take it out on him," she explained. "And then there are days when I'm so tired from dealing with the kids, I don't want to talk to anyone."

"Well, that gives us three things to think about," Ida Mae said.

"But you notice, Nick didn't talk either," Ren pointed out. "If Mary was the only one who was upset, Nick would have said *something*, wouldn't he?"

"And he called her 'honey' when he came in the door. He wouldn't do that if he was mad at her," Ida Mae said, feeling very pleased with herself.

"I don't know," Hannah said. "I'm so used to calling my husband 'sweetie,' I call him that automatically, even when I'm angry."

"So, we've basically just determined we know nothing," Ida Mae said, feeling her hope deflate like a leaky balloon. "I thought we were on to something."

"And you just might be," Hannah consoled. "I think it's safe to say they're both mad at each other and we'll find out why soon enough."

"How long does the silent treatment usually last?" Ren asked.

"It all depends."

"Well, let's get you back to your family," Ida Mae said. "I'm sorry nothing more exciting happened."

"That's okay. It felt good to be involved for a little while."

They took Hannah home and tried to pay Missy, but she refused, saying she'd had a good time and couldn't take money. The drive home was silent, Ida Mae mulling over everything that had happened, Ren no doubt thinking up some new invention.

"How long do you think we'll have to keep this up?" Ida Mae asked as they walked into the house.

"I hope not long," Ren said. "I'm as curious as all get-out to get to the bottom of this."

"If there's a bottom to get to," she replied. "We really don't have much to go on."

"But what do your guts tell you?"

"They tell me the Dunns are in over their heads," she said. "This is more than just marital discord. Something illegal is going on, I'm sure of it."

Chapter 7

The presidency took turns keeping an eye on the Dunns. For a whole week nothing much happened. Tansy reported that the baby had a diaper rash, but it cleared up quickly.

Ida Mae was beginning to wonder if they had imagined the whole thing. She concentrated on her other tasks, helped arrange a canned food drive, and kept an eye on Rose Hunter, who was due to be released from the hospital in a few days. She'd recovered nicely from her fall, and the doctors were pleased with her progress. Rose credited it all to Ida Mae's cookies.

Ren had added some new gadgets to his laptop. As they took their turn at the Dunns' that evening, he plinked away on the keyboard while Ida Mae immersed herself in the latest Whitney Award-winning novel.

Both of their heads snapped up as they saw a black car drive past, then slow and turn at the Dunns' gate.

"That was a Jaguar," Ren said, accentuating the "u" like a radio announcer. "Those things don't come cheap."

"I've never even seen one before," Ida Mae said.

Since the evening was unseasonably warm and bright, they decided to get out and take a little stroll to stretch their legs, but also to see what was going on. As they neared the turnoff to the Dunns', they slowed and took to the trees. Ida Mae was starting to give serious thought to Ren's previous suggestion of camouflage.

The Jaguar wasn't parked at the house.

"That's weird," Ren said. "Where'd the car go?"

"This is the only house down this lane," Ida Mae said. "They couldn't have been heading somewhere else."

"Stands to reason they'd have to come back this way. Why don't we watch for a minute and see what happens?"

They didn't have long to wait, as it turned out. Within minutes the Jaguar was back, coming from behind the house and up the lane. Ren and Ida Mae tried to see the driver from their concealed spot in the trees, but couldn't make out anything but a dirt-spattered license plate that lost a chunk of wet mud as it drove past them.

"What was the car doing behind the house?" Ren wondered.

"I think there's an old shed or something back there."

"Can we get to it if we keep to the trees?" Ren asked.

"I think so."

He checked his laptop—handy thing fit right under his arm. "Mary's in the living room right now, and Nick just came in. They're talking to each other, finally. They're going to sit down and watch a movie. If they stick to the living room and kitchen, we can't be seen. If they go into the bedrooms and happen to look a the window, we may be sunk."

"Well, let's get a move on while they're in the front part of the house."

They eased through the trees to the back of the property, the old shed placed much as Ida Mae remembered. They slipped out of the tree line and made their way to the door of the shed. Ren opened it slowly. Ida Mae shut her eyes tight, worried that the hinges would let out a screech and give them away, but the door opened silently.

It took a moment for Ida Mae's eyes to adjust to the dim, dusty light inside. Old rusty tools hung on the wall, and a push mower stood in the corner. Nothing else was in there.

Well, almost nothing.

Ren's shoe crunched as he stepped down. He backed up and stooped, picking up a foil hamburger wrapper between two fingers.

"This is from Wendy's," he said. "We don't have a Wendy's in Omni."

"And the Dunns don't eat meat," Ida Mae pointed out. "I bet whoever was in that Jaguar dropped this." She did not accentuate the 'u.'

Ren slid the wrapper into his pocket, heedless of any ketchup that might be on it. Ida Mae opened her mouth to warn him about possible stains, but then clamped it again. He was a grownup and did his own laundry. He could handle it.

When they met with the rest of the presidency the next morning, they all agreed they now had some evidence.

"Someone was in that shed, and I bet they weren't there just to eat a hamburger," Ida Mae said.

"How do we know it was a hamburger? Wendy's also makes a fine chicken sandwich," Arlette pointed out.

"That has nothing to do with it, Arlette! Someone drove onto the Dunns' property, went into the shed, and probably had a clandestine meeting with Nick. He wasn't in the house until after the Jaguar left. We heard him come in not long after the car drove away. He was probably meeting the driver."

"Did you make out any numbers on the plate?" Arlette asked.

"I couldn't. It was too muddy."

"The mud was wet?" Hannah leaned forward.

"Yes. A big chunk plopped off as it drove past us."

"The roads were completely dry yesterday," Hannah pointed out. "I went and did some errands and noticed that I even kicked up a little dust."

Ida Mae looked at Ren. "Did you see any mud back by the shed?"

"Not a speck."

"And was the rest of the car dirty?" Hannah asked.

"No. It was shiny."

"But what does that mean?" Tansy asked.

"I don't know," Ida Mae confessed. "Hannah, what does it mean?"

She leaned forward, her eyes alight. "Someone purposely found some mud and smeared it on the license plates."

"So no one could track them," Ida Mae added. "Genius."

"Well, not so genius if the rest of the car was clean," Hannah said. "It's pretty obvious they were just trying to hide the plates."

"Obvious to everyone but me," Ida Mae said, wondering how she could have missed something so simple. Hannah hadn't even been there, but she'd figured it out. "It's time to go the sheriff again."

○—

Ricky Shelton didn't even hide his disdain. "Ida Mae, you really need to find something better to do with your time. Doesn't the Relief Society keep you busy enough?"

"Oh, I'm very busy," she assured him. "We have a funeral tomorrow and some new move-ins arriving next week. Plus—"

"I didn't ask for a play-by-play of your daily activities," he said, pressing his eyelids with his fingertips. Ida Mae noticed how tired he looked. Probably up all night playing those video games his wife hated. "Listen, I appreciate the fact that the roads are dry and there isn't any mud. But did it occur to you that the car could have picked up the mud wherever they got the sandwich wrapper? And for that matter, maybe that wrapper was Nick's. It's not natural for a man to live without meat. I bet he eats burgers on the sly all the time, and just doesn't tell Mary to keep the peace."

"You don't present marriage in a very positive light, do you, Ricky?" Ida Mae wagged her finger at him.

"Playing video games, eating on the sly—just what do you think it means to be married?"

Ricky sat back, a pink hue creeping up his face. "Ida Mae, we're talking about your so-called evidence here. We're not analyzing my marriage, all right? Now, listen. Maybe the guy in the Jag drove back there, ate his sandwich, and drove back out. Maybe he brought a sandwich for Nick and they had themselves a nice little picnic in the shed. Maybe he smeared mud on the plates so Mary wouldn't know who to blame for the secret hamburger. I don't know, Ida Mae, and I don't care. It is not illegal to eat meat, okay? Now, listen. Go take care of your funeral. Knit some leper bandages or whatever it is you do."

"Crochet," Ida Mae interjected.

"Knit, crochet, I don't care. Just let me get back to work and stop bothering me with hamburger wrappers."

"Arlette said it could have been a chicken sandwich," she added.

Ricky took a deep breath, then let it out slowly. "I don't care what kind of sandwich it was, Ida Mae. There is no evidence of any wrong doing, and you need to let me get back to work. We've got a vandal at the elementary school, and I have work to do."

Ida Mae walked out of the office, irate and indignant. What was the world coming to when you couldn't count on law enforcement to keep you safe? Dismissing the wrapper, not understanding the significance of the mud—it was clearer to her than ever that they were on their own. She might have doubted the wisdom of this project to begin with, but not any more.

Chapter 8

"The older I get, the crankier I am," Rose Hunter said, reaching for another cookie off the fresh plate Ida Mae had brought in. "I'm getting to where I can hardly stand myself."

"I think we all go through that from time to time," Ida Mae said, knowing exactly what Rose meant. She didn't know what she would have done if Ren hadn't moved back in—he kept her from spending too much time alone with herself. He also kept involving her in illegal covert activity, but she'd overlook that for the sake of the good company he provided. He also got free movie rentals at work, and she'd finally gotten her hands on "Becoming Jane." There were definitely advantages.

"I just hate to think what I'm putting Heidi through," Rose said, interrupting one of Ida Mae's typical imaginative lapses—that James McAvoy was a good actor. "I think Reed's hair is getting thinner, too."

"I'm sure we can get it all worked out," Ida Mae said, pulling herself by force back into the conversation. "I'll go talk to Heidi and see how things are over there."

"Well, when they release me tomorrow, I don't think she'll be excited to have me back," Rose said, taking another cookie. "What kind is this, anyway? I've eaten four now."

"That's a sour cream coconut chocolate chip. My mother's recipe."

"Well, if my mother cooked like this, I think my father would have eaten out a little less," Rose said. "Are you trying to fatten me up?"

"You certainly could use it. I bet a sneeze would blow you over."

"I wouldn't try it if I were you." Rose wiped her mouth with a tissue. "If you would go talk to Heidi, I'd appreciate it. I've tried, but she still acts skittish around me."

"Consider it done." Ida Mae had two more plates of cookies out in the car, and she knew she'd find a place for them to go. Tansy and Arlette had a full two dozen keeping them company out at the Dunns' this afternoon. Good thing that recipe made so many.

An hour later, she strode briskly up the walk to the Hunters' door, noting the peeling paint on the eaves. Heaven knew Reed was a busy man, but if he wanted to keep his property value up—she bit the inside of her lip. She'd try again. *My, how nice the evergreen bushes on either side of the door look. They're so . . . green.* She winced at her sad attempt to be positive, but it was the best she could do at that moment.

Heidi opened the door, her eyes going wide at the sight of the plate in Ida Mae's hands. "Come in, Sister Babbitt. You didn't have to bring me anything, although I won't turn them down."

Ida Mae relinquished the plate and stepped into the spacious foyer. "I've just come from the hospital," she said, shucking off her coat. "Rose's terribly worried right now."

"What about?" Heidi grabbed Ida Mae's coat with her free hand, not—Ida Mae noticed—loosening her grip on that plate.

"She feels she's a burden to you. She knows she's added to your plate." Ida Mae winced at her unconscious choice of words, but Heidi didn't seem to notice.

"To be honest, Sister Babbitt, I'm not the care-giving type. I fall apart if any of the kids get sick. Reed gets a hang nail and I'm in tears. I don't know how to nurture. And now, with Mother Hunter needing a little extra care, I'm so stressed just thinking about it, I don't know what to do."

"You can start by sitting down and having a cookie," Ida Mae said, motioning toward the couch. Heidi sat down, her very carriage indicating the stress she was under. With her mouth full of cookie, a tear rolled down her cheek, and Ida Mae pulled a new package of pocket-sized Kleenex out of her purse.

"I'm sorry to be such a bawl-baby," Heidi said, sniffling loudly. Ida Mae offered the Kleenex a little more pointedly, and Heidi finally took the hint and accepted a tissue. "But it's this whole Mormon woman thing. Aren't we all supposed to be the perfect housekeepers, the perfect nurturers, the ones who hold it all together? It's all I can do to keep the dishes done, and anything else on top of that is just too much for me to handle."

Ida Mae sat back and pondered for a moment. "You know what, Heidi, I don't think that any woman on earth measures up to this 'perfect Mormon woman' image we've all got in our heads. I don't even know what started that nasty rumor in the first place. I don't think we're supposed to be perfect about everything all the time—I just think we're supposed to be the very best we can be.

"Take, for instance, DeeDee Wheeler. She has a lovely singing voice and has been working to cultivate it. It's not a perfect voice, but she's making the most of it and using it to bless those around her. At the same time, she's not as good a cook as Iris Standing, but she's learning new recipes and asking the other sisters for advice. There's no such thing as perfection. We're just working with what we've been given and forging on, every day. The main thing is that we don't give up."

"I feel like that's what I've done," Heidi said. "The twins run me ragged every day, and . . . you don't know this yet, because we've just been told ourselves, but it turns out that Tommy is deaf."

"Oh, no!" Ida Mae looked down at the floor, where the two-year-old played with cars. She noticed, for the first time, that he wasn't making the typical car-crash noises little boys like to make. He was silent. "I'm so sorry to hear that."

Heidi reached for two more cookies and handed one to Tommy. "It's been a blow. I'm still in shock, and Reed has totally withdrawn from the situation. We're going to talk to specialists to see if there's anything we can do, and we'll be taking sign language classes and teaching him to lip-read." She took a huge bite and barely chewed before swallowing. "I know a hearing-impaired person can live a wonderful, rich life and achieve everything they want to, but I'm worried about his safety. I don't want him to wander out in the road and not hear an approaching car."

Ida Mae reached out and patted her hand. "I don't even know what to say. This will certainly be a challenge."

"Am I selfish to feel like I can't handle Reed's mother right now? We're the only ones with a house big enough to accommodate her. I don't work out of the home, so it seems like I'm the perfect candidate. But I'm drowning, Sister Babbitt. I'm absolutely drowning."

To accentuate her statement, the tears started to flow again. Ida Mae sat quietly while Heidi had her cry-out, her mind working furiously.

Service was a wonderful thing. Christ-like compassion for others was one of the greatest attributes she could name. But was it right for Heidi to feel so burdened because of it? Was it right for Rose to feel like an inconvenience? Were everyone's needs being met by this situation? She just didn't think they were.

"Does Rose know about Tommy?" she asked.

Heidi shook her head. "We only got the final diagnosis this morning. I was planning to go tell her this afternoon."

This news would surely devastate Rose and make her feel more like an intruder. That just wasn't fair— she deserved to live joyfully.

"Let me think some things over, Heidi," she said, knocking around an idea in her brain. "You told me a while back that she said she'd go live in a care center?"

Heidi sat up straight. "That's what she said, but I won't hear of it. It just seems wrong to send her out to pasture when we're right here and can take care of her."

Ida Mae held up a hand. "I wasn't saying you should send her off somewhere. I was asking if she had the means to afford to live somewhere."

"Yes, she does. She has a good monthly income."

"That's what I needed to know," Ida Mae said. Heidi visibly relaxed, although her back was still stiff.

"Now, I have another surprise for you, in addition to the cookies." Ida Mae reached into her purse and pulled out a jar of bath salts. "These are the best for soaking out stiff muscles. I want you to go upstairs, run a bath, and soak for a good hour. I'm going to stay down here and play with Tommy."

Heidi blinked. "Oh, I don't know, Sister Babbitt. That seems like such an imposition."

"I'm suggesting it. How can it be an imposition?"

Heidi looked down at Tommy, then back at Ida Mae. "Okay. You're on."

She disappeared, and Ida Mae heard the bath water start up. She nodded. That ought to help, at least a little.

She looked down at Tommy, at the golden ringlets that covered his head. He was a beautiful child—he looked like he should be on the front of a Valentine card. She got up and painfully lowered herself onto her knees so she could look at his cars. He glanced up at her, gave her a sweet smile, and handed her a blue truck.

They played cars together for the better part of an hour. When Heidi reentered the room, her hair still damp, she looked like a whole new woman.

"I haven't just relaxed in—I don't know how long," she said, sinking into a chair. "Thank you for giving me this time to myself, Sister Babbitt."

"You needed it, and we had a wonderful time, didn't we, Tommy?" She touched the child's head, and he leaned over to give her a hug. "You know, with his temperament, I think he'll accept his lot in life with a good attitude. I can see him really tackling this challenge and conquering it."

"I think you're right," Heidi said. "He doesn't seem to have an angry temper. Maybe he'll be able to deal with his frustrations better than I would, for instance."

"And, because he's so young, he may not have that frustration," Ida Mae continued. "You can't miss something you've never had, and if he's taught how to communicate, maybe it won't be as difficult as you're thinking it might."

"I'll try to stay positive," Heidi said. "You've been a lifesaver today, Sister Babbitt. Thank you."

"You are most welcome. Now, I wonder if you'd do something for me."

"I would love to. What do you need?"

"Will you give me a hand off this floor?"

Heidi bent down and tucked a hand under Ida Mae's elbow. After regaining her footing, and turning an altogether unflattering shade of pink, Ida Mae picked up her purse. "I'm going to give your situation some thought, Heidi, but I'm sure we'll be able to find a way. This life is about finding joy even while being tested. Let's find you some joy."

"Thank you, Sister Babbitt. I really appreciate that."

I wonder, Ida Mae thought as she walked to her car. *I wonder if there's a way to make it work . . .*

Chapter 9

"T his week has been duller than dishwater," Arlette proclaimed, jabbing her knitting needle into her ball of magenta yarn. Honestly, why the woman couldn't choose better colors, Ida Mae simply didn't know. She pulled her brain back before heading too far down that track and concentrated on the meeting at hand. "Nothing has been happening out at the Dunns'. Not one thing. Unless you count the fact that the baby took his first steps."

Everyone in the room oooh'd and ahhh'd at that until Ida Mae brought the meeting back to order.

"On other fronts, the bishop's blood pressure is down another two points, and his wife is feeling somewhat better, although the doctor doesn't want her up and around. He wants her flat down until the birth."

"Remind me when she's due?" Tansy asked.

"In two months," Hannah said, checking her notes. "But they think she may come early, what with it being triplets and all."

"Her sister is still there and is planning to stay until after the birth, but they do need someone to sit with the children while the sister gets the grocery shopping done and what-not."

"Someone should go over and let the sister have a break," Tansy said. "I saw her at church on Sunday, and the poor thing looked tired to death."

"What's her name?" Arlette asked. "We can't just keep calling her 'the sister.'"

"Her name is Janet," Ida Mae said. "She's single and lives in Idaho. Her coming at this time is a blessing."

"Do we have a volunteer list?" Arlette asked, and Hannah pulled one out of her folder.

"Looks like we're covered for help and dinner until Thursday," Ida Mae said. "I'll go over Thursday night and take dinner and send Janet out for the evening. The bishop has interviews at the church that night, so they'll need a sitter."

"That's good of you, Ida Mae," Tansy said. "Let's see—I'll go sit with them on Saturday afternoon."

They worked out a schedule for the Sylvesters, then turned the conversation back to the Dunns. "Ren's at work, but he told me to put him down for evenings this week," Ida Mae said. "He's mostly working mornings and afternoons these days."

"Thankfully," Arlette added. "I hate sitting out there in the dark."

"Do you really think we'll find out anything?" Tansy said. "We've been waiting for such a long time now."

"It hasn't been that long," Ida Mae reminded her. "It only seems that way because we're anxious."

The phone rang, and Ida Mae rose to get it.

"Sister Babbitt? This is Hannah's husband. Is she still there?" Ned's usual calm voice was contorted. "I need to talk to her."

"I'll get her for you."

Ida Mae took the phone into the living room and handed it to her secretary, who listened for a moment and turned a shade of green.

"I have to go," she said, hanging up. "Joey was just hit by a car."

○—

Tansy sat on one side of Hannah with Ida Mae on the other. Arlette had gone down to the cafeteria to scare up some juice, and Ned paced the waiting room while he talked.

"I was going to the store," he said, running a hand through his hair. "I put the children in their car seats and got them all buckled in. We went into the store—we were fine. Everything was just fine." His voice broke, and he stopped pacing to stand by the window. "When we got back out to the car, the cart hit a slippery patch and started to roll. I grabbed it, but Joey must have thought we were still walking, and he went on ahead. I called out to him, but just then a car started to back out and didn't see him."

Hannah shuddered. "I never should have sent you to the store. I should have gone myself, on the way home from the meeting. That way, the children would have been safe at home."

"You don't blame me for this, do you?" Ned turned to her, his eyes filled with anguish. "I was careful, Hannah. I swear it."

"No, I don't blame you. It's just—children and parking lots don't mix. That's why I like to shop without them. It's so much safer."

"It's impossible to keep children safe every minute of every day," Ida Mae pointed out. "If it's not a car, it's a hot stove or a bottle of medicine or a sharp corner or a kitchen knife. They will find something to hurt themselves on, no matter what we do."

"I should have put Joey in the cart too," Ned said,

apparently not hearing what Ida Mae was trying to explain. "If he'd been in the cart, this never would have happened."

"We don't know that," Ida Mae said. "What if you hadn't been able to catch the cart, and the car hit the whole thing with both children in it?"

Ned flinched. "I'm not sure if you're trying to comfort me or make me feel worse, Sister Babbitt."

"I'm not trying to hurt you, Ned. I'm just pointing out that it could have been worse. The car was going slowly, so we're only looking at a broken leg. They're fixing it right now. There's so much to be grateful for." She gave Hannah's arm a squeeze.

"You're right. I'm sorry." Ned sat down finally, resting his elbows on his knees. "I just can't stop seeing it, you know?"

Arlette came in and pushed a bottle of orange juice into his hands. "I bet you didn't have any breakfast."

"You're right—it was crazy this morning." He downed the juice in one long series of swigs.

"Now, your mother has the baby?" Ida Mae asked Hannah.

"Yes. She'll keep Jeremiah as long as we need."

"All right then, you just concentrate on Joey. The doctor said the surgery should be over by two. Let's go get the both of you some food."

"I'll stay here in case there's any word," Arlette said, sitting down and pulling out her yarn.

With some encouragement, both Hannah and Ned ate some food from the hospital cafeteria. Ida Mae and Tansy watched carefully to make sure they got enough to keep them going.

"Ned says you have good insurance," Ida Mae said to Hannah. "Everything is going to be fine."

"I know," Hannah said, no life in her voice. "But when does the 'fine' start?"

Ida Mae pulled the girl into a hug. "I don't know, but it has to be soon," she said into Hannah's hair. "All happily-ever-afters start somewhere."

○—

Ida Mae pulled back her sage green comforter and crawled into bed, feeling like what's left on the road after the snow plow goes by. Her heart ached for Hannah and Ned—the surgery was a success and Joey would be walking around again soon, but the trauma of the event would forever be burned on their brains. She couldn't even imagine what Ned had gone through, seeing his son in that situation.

Ren had nothing to report after his stint at the Dunns', and Ida Mae wondered if all the really good stuff was happening late at night, after they'd given up. Maybe there was a way to rig some sort of gizmo that was powerful enough to transmit from the Dunns' all the way to her own house. She'd have to ask Ren in the morning.

She reached out to her bedside table and picked up her daily planner. Tomorrow—what was tomorrow? Ah, Wednesday. The day had stretched on for so long, it seemed as though it ought to be Friday by now.

It was Sister Reynolds' birthday, and also Sister Plummer's. She had their small gifts ready, sitting on the shelf in the hall, so that was one less thing to do. She needed to call around for the best price on inflated balloons for a Relief Society party later in the month—Hannah was going to, but she relieved Hannah of all responsibilities for the next couple of weeks. She made a note to think about Heidi's situation and to buy some ingredients for the Sylvesters' dinner on Thursday. After jotting down a few more words, she closed her book and turned off the lamp, sinking into the pillow.

Her calling was so much more than a to-do list. Behind every task she performed were real people, real trials and feelings. Some days, she tried to depersonalize so she could move forward without getting overwhelmed, but those days never went as well as the days when she threw herself into her calling heart and soul. Yes, she got overwhelmed, but she always found the strength she needed to keep moving. The errand of angels was given to women, but the angels didn't just turn the job over and leave. They stuck around and did whatever they could to help.

Chapter 10

Janet walked in the door looking ten years younger.

"Did you have a good time?" Ida Mae asked, glancing up from the dinner dishes she was washing.

"I really did, Sister Babbitt. Thank you." Janet took off her coat and slung it over the back of a kitchen chair, completely heedless of the fact that Ida Mae had just cleaned the kitchen until it shone and the coat was the start of a whole new pile of mess. Ida Mae took a deep breath. Janet was tired. She would overlook the coat.

"How were the children?"

"Oh, we had a wonderful time. We played games, and they went to bed pretty easily." She hadn't repeated her mistake of getting down on the floor. She doubted her body would ever touch a floor again, unless she passed out and fell on it, which wasn't entirely out of the question, given how tired she was. "They are a frisky bunch, aren't they?"

"Yes, they are. But every one of them is as good as gold."

Ida Mae dried her hands on a dish towel, then carefully hung it on the oven door. "I put the leftovers in the fridge, and Sister Sylvester's book stack has been replenished. I even had Ren bring her some new movies to watch."

"Thank you so much, Sister Babbitt. I don't know what we'd do without the Relief Society."

Ida Mae didn't know either—but of one thing she was sure. If it weren't for the Relief Society, she wouldn't be facing a possible jail term. Well, she couldn't blame the Relief Society for that—she blamed Ren. She said good night, stuck her head in to tell Sister Sylvester goodbye, then went to meet that young man out by the Dunns' house.

○━

"So, I was thinking, is there any kind of alarm or something you could rig to warn us when someone is approaching the house?"

Ren looked at her with new respect. "You've been giving this some thought, Auntie."

"Well, I had a lot of time to think while I was waiting for Ethan Sylvester to let go of his sister's hair."

"Did you tickle him in the armpits?"

"I did. That child has a will of iron."

"Let me think on it for a little while. We don't want something that would go off every single time someone went near the house—we'd be picking up any stray cat or door-to-door salesman, too."

"What about another camera? A stronger one, posted outside."

He stroked the faint stubble that grew along his jawline. He'd been working on it for several days and it hadn't changed a bit. She hated to tell him, but she sensed he already knew. He'd checked it out five times in the rearview mirror already and they'd only been parked an hour.

"I'll think on that. It would have to be a lot stronger, you know, and . . ."

His voice trailed off, and she could almost hear the gears in his head turning. He was a smart boy—she had no doubt he'd have a new invention to show her within the next day or two.

Headlights appeared on the road behind them, and they tensed as a black Jaguar passed, then slowed to turn into the Dunns' driveway.

"This is our chance," Ren said, opening his door.

"Chance to do what?"

"To really spy."

What had they been doing up until that point? Ida Mae nearly asked the question, but Ren was already creeping through the woods, and she didn't want to be left behind. She got out too, closing her door softly, as he had done, and caught up to him.

They edged through the trees until they came to the clearing where the shed stood. Sure enough, the black car was parked there, the driver waiting, still inside. He struck a match and lit up a cigarette, flicking the match out his window. Ida Mae could see the glow of the match as it hit the ground, then snuffed out.

"Well, of all the—" she began, but Ren shushed her.

"He could have started a forest fire!" she protested. "These trees aren't fake, you know."

"You want him to hear you?" he hissed in her ear, and she shushed.

A few minutes later, Nick came out of the house and crossed the hundred yards to the shed. Ren and Ida Mae moved farther back into the shadows. Her heart was beating so fast, it almost hurt.

"I've got to be quick," Nick said. "My wife thinks I just came out to grab the mail."

"And so you did." The man inside the car handed

him an envelope. "Same as before, but with a little extra for good behavior."

Nick took the envelope and turned it over in his hands. "Don't you think you could tell me what's going on now?" he asked.

"The less you know, the better," the driver said. "Trust me. Go back inside."

Nick turned and walked toward the house, pausing at the front to collect the real mail. Ren and Ida Mae stayed hidden until the car was long gone, just in case.

Once back in Ren's car, Ida Mae took a deep breath. "That was something else," she said. "I thought for sure one of them was going to see us."

"It's pitch black out here," Ren said. "They couldn't see a thing."

She rummaged through the sack at their feet and pulled out an A&W. She felt a little better after taking a long gulp, although she was sure the carbonation wasn't doing a thing for her. Arlette would have something to say about it, but Arlette wasn't there.

"Let's keep a chart of when the man in the black car comes," she suggested. "Maybe there's a pattern."

"Good idea," Ren said. "Why don't you write down what we know so far, and I'll get to work on that long range camera."

Before leaving, they watched the kitchen camera and listened to the bug to see if everything was all right. Nick didn't mention anything to his wife about the envelope.

"He said he doesn't know what's going on," Ida Mae said as they pulled into their own driveway. "That makes me feel a little better. Maybe he's innocent."

"He's not totally innocent," Ren said. "Even if he doesn't know exactly what's up, he's got to know that *something* is going on. He's an accomplice, either way."

"I know." She sighed. "I just hate to think what will happen when all this comes out. Poor Mary. Poor children."

"There's still a chance this is all just a big misunderstanding," Ren said.

"Not likely. The man in the car reminded me of the Godfather."

"Why?"

"I don't know. He just did."

Ida Mae pondered that question as she fell asleep that night. Just what was it about that man that reminded her of a mobster? She hit on the answer right before she fell asleep. The arm that held out the envelope was encased in a dark suit. That's what it was. Now, she realized it wasn't a crime to wear a suit, but late on a Thursday night? To a meeting in the woods? That was a little odd indeed.

Chapter 11

I'm sorry for the mess," Hannah said, pushing a laundry basket to the side with her foot. Her baby sat on her hip, a chubby fist grasping Hannah's hair with a death grip.

"You're not to worry," Ida Mae said, scooting a toy off the couch and taking a seat. "I've seen worse than this in my own house."

"Not since your children grew up, I'd bet." Hannah put the baby in the playpen and sat across from Ida Mae, tucking her newly freed hair behind her ear.

"It has been a little while, that's for sure." Ida Mae glanced around. Hannah's house was always clean—she knew the girl worked hard on that, but it was also always slightly cluttered, a state she knew caused Hannah untold grief. A sprinkling of Cheerios on the end table was nothing to have a canary about. Now, if the Cheerios were from last week, for instance, then *that* would be a worry.

"Now, I've come to talk with you about a few things," Ida Mae said.

"I'm sorry about having to take a break from my calling," Hannah said, leaping in. "I'll be back on top of things before you know it."

Ida Mae held up a hand. "You're not even to worry about that. How is Joey?"

"A little sleepy from the pain medication. He's napping right now, but the doctor thinks he'll make a full recovery, and soon. Children his age heal quickly."

"It's a good thing they do, with all the trouble they get into." She shifted a little on the couch. "I think I may have an answer to your rental problem."

"You do?"

"Yes, I do. But it's a little bit unconventional."

Hannah cocked her head to the side. "What do you mean?"

"Rose Hunter was released from the hospital the other day. You know she's been living with Reed and Heidi, but she feels like a burden, and she really can't live on her own anymore. Heidi is going through a rough time—Tommy was just diagnosed as being deaf, and she's a wreck trying to keep up with everything."

"Oh, no," Hannah said. "That's so sad."

"I have a proposition. How much is the rent for your basement apartment?"

"Five hundred a month."

"Well, I've been talking to Reed, and he's willing to pay you seven hundred and fifty dollars if you would rent the apartment to his mother and make sure she gets her medicine every day. She also needs someone to check on her three or four times daily to make sure she's all right. He's arranged for a nurse to come in and bathe her and prepare her lunch, and she's signed up for Meals on Wheels for her dinner. She just likes cold cereal in the morning and can get it herself, so there won't be any breakfast to worry about."

Hannah blinked. "Seven hundred and fifty, just to check on Sister Hunter? That's all I'd have to do?"

"That's it."

"But what about the children? Sometimes they're a little noisy, and I wouldn't want to disturb her."

"Rose is a good woman, and she raised a passel of her own children. I think she'll be very agreeable."

Hannah shook her head. "I don't know what to say."

"Do you think it would work out for you? It wouldn't take you away from the children too much?"

"I don't think so," Hannah said. "But can Reed really afford it? I mean, the rent, but also the nurse and everything?"

"Actually, a lot of it would be covered by Rose. She was left quite a wealthy widow and can afford the things she needs. Besides, a nursing home would charge at least two thousand a month, and this won't run that high. It will be a savings."

"Can she get around on her own, then?"

"She can move fairly well, and she has a walker now." Ida Mae noticed the spots of pink that had appeared in Hannah's cheeks, but she couldn't tell if they were good spots or bad spots. "What do you think?"

"I think it sounds good," Hannah said. "Let me talk it over with Ned—he was saying that he needed to fix a few small things down there. I don't know how long that will take, but I'll ask him and we'll get back to you."

Ida Mae nodded. "That sounds like a good idea."

She took a deep breath of the crystalline air as she walked out to her car. She had a good feeling about this arrangement. Rose didn't want to feel like a burden, and she felt even more like one since finding out about Tommy. Living in Hannah's basement would help her feel more independent, yet if she needed anything at all, help was right there. Reed had suggested an intercom system, and Ida Mae thought it was a wonderful idea. She'd mention it to Hannah after the girl had a chance to think things over.

Chapter 12

The Secret Sisters, as Tansy persisted in calling them, were gathered around Ida Mae's kitchen table. Ida Mae had taken the responsibility of writing down everything they knew, including the dates and times they had discovered something odd at the Dunns'. She had also taken the responsibility of making a plate of brownies, and since no one objected to either action, she figured she'd done the right thing.

"Thanks for inviting me to this meeting of the Blue-Haired Ladies," Ren said, reaching for a brownie.

"We most certainly do not have blue hair," Arlette objected at the same time Tansy said, "Where would we be without you, Ren?"

"It's just an expression," Ren said to Arlette, wisely choosing to head off the argument before it started.

"It means, ladies of slightly advanced years. It's a compliment. It refers to your wisdom."

"Well, how would you like being compared to a Muppet?" Arlette shot back.

Ida Mae held up her hands. "Let's get back on topic," she said. "I'm a little lost on details without Hannah, but I think I've remembered the big stuff. Please look my chart over and see if there are any holes, all right?" She waited as the room grew silent with reading.

"It looks about right to me," Tansy said at last, taking a brownie. Arlette and Ren nodded their agreement.

"There are a couple of questions that came to mind while I was compiling this list." Ida Mae pulled out her notebook and flipped to the page where she had written down her thoughts. "First off, just where is it that Nick does . . . whatever he's doing? He's not doing it at home—all we've seen is the drop-off of payment for the job. Where is he doing this job?"

Everyone nodded. "That's good thinking, Ida Mae," Arlette said, a hint of admiration in her voice.

"And, in addition to that, where is he all day? Did he really find a job and is doing this other thing on the side, or is he just leaving for the day to make Mary *think* he's found a job? For that matter, just how much does Mary know?"

"I don't think she knows a whole lot," Ren spoke up. "Nick isn't even sure what's going on—how would Mary know more than Nick?"

"True, true." Ida Mae made a note on her pad. "I believe our next step is to follow Nick. See where he goes during the day."

"I just gassed up my van," Arlette said, knitting needles aquiver.

"Actually, I was thinking we should send Ren," Ida Mae said. "Nick knows all of us by sight from church. He's never met Ren."

"Yeah, inactive member that I am," Ren said.

"Who knew your inactivity would come so in handy?" Tansy said brightly, always ready to find the positive in a situation.

"Ren, when is your next day off?"

Ren pulled a piece of paper out of his pocket and consulted it. "Tomorrow, actually."

"Okay, great. Do we have any idea when Nick leaves the house for the day?"

No one knew, so Ida Mae proposed that Ren be in position around 6 a.m. just to be on the safe side. "I'll make you a good breakfast before you go," she promised before he could raise an objection, and, as she'd hoped, that squelched his protest.

"In the meantime, let's keep to our posts so we don't miss anything."

The meeting essentially concluded, the rest of the brownies disappeared, and the group trickled out of the house. Ida Mae placed a call to Reed and Heidi to see if she could swing by the next day, and then she called Hannah.

"How is Joey doing?" she asked.

"He's all right, I guess. He's in a lot of pain still." Ida Mae could hear the tiredness in Hannah's voice. "They said it would be a little while, so we're trying to be patient."

"And what do you need, dear?"

"I need a nap." Hannah tacked on a chuckle, but Ida Mae could tell she was serious.

"I'll be over in half an hour."

"Oh, you don't need to do that," Hannah protested.

"Yes, I do. I'll be there in half an hour, and you're going to bed early. What time does your husband get home?"

"One thirty. He's still on the late shift."

"Then I'll stay until he gets there."

Hannah tried to protest again, but Ida Mae wouldn't let her.

"We need you, Hannah. I tried to take notes and make sense of them, and I'm terrible at it. What am I going to do if you get sick from exhaustion and it takes you longer to come back to me?"

"Well, if you're sure . . ."

"I'm more than sure. I'll be there."

Ida Mae hung up and grabbed her purse. She shoved her book, her journal, and a pen inside, then rummaged through her cupboards for some good snacks. She changed the laundry from the washer to the dryer and watered her plants, and was all set to go when the phone rang.

"Sister Babbitt? This is Marsha DeLong. Is it too late for me to call?"

"Of course not," she said, glancing at the clock. Well, it *was* a little late, but she had just called the Hunters and Hannah, so she couldn't be too critical. "What can I do for you?"

"Well, I was out doing my visiting teaching this afternoon, and you know how we're supposed to report things we think you should know?"

Ida Mae pressed her lips together. This was how they got involved with the Dunns'. "Yes?"

"Well, Darcy Gimble has gotten herself into some trouble. I mean, trouble. You know what I mean." Marsha lowered her voice until Ida Mae could hardly hear her. "She's pregnant."

Darcy was nearly eighteen and the Laurel president. Ida Mae was greatly surprised at the news.

"Darcy? Are you sure?"

"I'm sure, Sister Babbitt. Sister Gimble told me about it—they'd just found out. She was in tears."

Ida Mae's head was spinning. She'd worked with Darcy on various projects and thought that, of anyone, that girl had her head on straight. "I'll go over tomorrow," she promised, jotting a note on her calendar.

"Thank you, Sister Babbitt. I know Sister Gimble would appreciate the visit."

Ida Mae threw on her coat and walked out to her car. Darcy Gimble, pregnant. She never would have dreamed it. Becky Patterson, yes. Wendy Markum, definitely. But not Darcy.

She brought herself up short as she climbed into the car. She had no right to judge Becky and Wendy like that. Sure, the girls weren't very active, and they exhibited behavior that wasn't in accordance with Church teachings, but how did she know what they were thinking and feeling? How did she know they were destined for teen pregnancy—she couldn't read their minds. She felt immediately ashamed of herself.

"I'm sorry," she prayed aloud. "I shouldn't judge like that. I was just so surprised about Darcy."

She pulled out of her driveway, her thoughts skittering all over the place. Darcy's mother was so proud of her grades—she'd been telling Ida Mae just last month that Darcy was getting ready to start applying for scholarships. The girl never dressed immodestly. She was just the ideal teenager in every way.

Then Ida Mae had a thought that struck her even more forcefully than her judgment of Becky and Wendy. She pulled over to the side of the road, unable to concentrate because of the way her mind was tingling.

She had no right to judge Darcy positively any more than she had the right to judge the other two girls negatively.

Didn't the scripture say, "Judge not?" It didn't say, "Judge not negatively." It was just a plain, blanket statement—"Judge not."

Sure, Darcy was a "good girl." No one ever worried about her because she was good. But in labeling her that way, was it possible that her needs had been overlooked? Had they been so busy shepherding the "lost sheep" that they forgot to feed the ones in the pen?

Tears rolled Ida Mae's cheeks. She felt thoroughly ashamed of herself. True, her calling did involve a lot of running around to put out fires. Emergencies always came first. And, sometimes, there were so many emergencies, it seemed like she did nothing else. She remembered the old saying about the squeaky wheel getting the grease. How many wheels were suffering in silence?

"Forgive me," she prayed again, this time with all her heart. Never again would she judge someone to be above needing love and support.

○—

Hannah's house was quiet when she arrived. "The children are asleep," Hannah said, "but Joey will wake up soon for his next pill. Poor thing—he can only sleep for a little bit at a time, and he has to take a pain pill every four hours."

"Where is his pill?"

Hannah showed her where the bottle was.

"He should take it at midnight. If he wakes up before then, get him a drink and make him comfortable until then, okay? We have to be careful not to dose him too frequently."

"Okay."

"And his leg needs to stay up on the pillow that's in there. He keeps wiggling off, but it needs to stay elevated."

"Sounds pretty typical, a five-year-old being wiggly. Now, you go lie down. You look all worn out."

Hannah offered her a grim smile. "Thank you. This means a lot."

Silence fell over the house, and Ida Mae settled into the easy chair in the corner by the fireplace. She pulled out her book and begin to read, just reaching the part where the main suspect was getting ready to make a phone call to accomplices unknown when she heard Joey start to cry. Glancing at the clock and seeing that it was only ten, she moved quickly into his bedroom, hoping to soothe him before Hannah woke up.

"Hi, Joey," she said, peeking in.

"Hi, Sister Rabbit," he said. She'd tried to correct him in a half-hearted way once, but found his nickname for her so endearing, she couldn't insist.

"Your mommy is taking a nap, so I'm going to watch you, okay?"

"Okay." Tears were lined up on his cheek, and he wiped them away with his pajama sleeve. "My leg hurts."

"I bet it does, sweetie." She helped him put it back up on the pillow, then glanced around the room, wondering what she could do to amuse him for two hours. "Are you sleepy?" Maybe he'd go back down until midnight.

"No."

Well, there went *that* bright idea.

Her eye fell on a bookcase. "Should I read you a story?"

"Okay."

"Which one?"

He pointed. "Thomas."

She pulled the blue and black book of the shelf. "Thomas and Friends. I don't think I've ever read this one." She took a seat next to the bed and read him the story.

"Now Barney," he said.

The next hour ticked by. She read every single book on his shelf and was about to start again when she noticed he had fallen asleep. It was eleven fifteen. Only forty-five minutes to go. She put his leg back up on the pillow and tucked him in.

She'd never had a broken leg, but she could imagine what it must feel like. Poor little guy.

At ten after midnight he woke up, and she gave him the pain pill. He fell asleep after a few minutes, and she went back into the living room, her hand to her forehead. She felt like she could use one of those pills too—her head was killing her. How was Hannah coping with all this and a baby, too?

Ned came home right on time and thanked her profusely.

"It was my pleasure," she told him, embellishing the truth just a little. The experience hadn't been bad in any way—it was just the worry for the child that made it difficult. She drove home in a bit of a fog, briefly wondering why she seemed to be doing so much child care lately. Could she call a babysitting specialist to work in the Relief Society? That might take a load off, if there really was such a calling. She'd have to ask.

Chapter 13

The phone rang first thing in the morning. Ida Mae reached for it, missing it on the first grab. She should have left it in the hall instead of bringing it into the bedroom—she hated answering the phone half-asleep.

"Hello?" she mumbled when she finally had the instrument in her hand.

"Ida Mae? It's after eight o'clock. Are you still in bed?"

"Good morning, Arlette. I was out living the wild life last night and came home drunk."

"I don't find that amusing, Ida Mae."

"Sorry." *No, I'm not,* Ida Mae thought. *Call me at the crack of dawn, expect me to be cheerful, and see what you get.*

"I just wanted to see if Ren got out the door safely."

Ida Mae sat up like a shot, fully awake. She was supposed to get up and make him a good breakfast that morning. It had been part of the deal.

"I'm sure he did," she said, pressing a hand to her head. "I overslept, what with this hangover and all."

"Really, Ida Mae. I'll call back later when you aren't feeling so fractious."

Ida Mae hung up the phone and climbed out of bed. Had Ren already gone, or was he counting on her to wake him up? His bed was empty and somewhat made, and as she walked into the kitchen, her eyes fell on a note propped up on the table.

> *I didn't know you could snore like that, Auntie. I came in to check on you at 5:30 and thought you'd swallowed a truck. See you later, and don't worry about me. I ate.*

Ida Mae smiled, then threw a bagel in the toaster. She might not have swallowed a truck, but she felt like she'd been hit by one. She'd been back to her house by two that morning, but she'd lain awake another hour, wondering if there wasn't anything else they could do for Hannah. She'd call some of the ladies in the ward and see if they couldn't go in and spell her more in the evenings.

Dressed in her lavender velour pantsuit and feeling much better after her shower, Ida Mae headed over to the Hunters'. Heidi greeted her at the door, and they went into the living room where Reed and Rose waited on the leather couch.

"I believe I may have a solution to your difficulty," Ida Mae said, coming straight to the point, as was her typical style. She saw no reason to beat around the bush when the bush was on her timecard. "Rose, do you know Hannah Eyre?"

"The blonde with the two small boys? I've noticed her at church."

Ida Mae glanced at Reed. She'd already talked the whole thing over with him, but she wasn't sure how Rose would take to the idea. "Well, she has a basement apartment that's just adorable. It's a walkout, so there aren't any stairs, and it's got a lot of sunlight. It's one bedroom, one bath, and fully furnished. She's been trying to rent it out, but everyone seems to want two bedrooms these days. What would you think of going to live there?"

Rose glanced at Reed. "You already know about this, don't you?"

"I do. I think it's a good idea, Mama. It would give you the space you need, but you'd also have someone handy if you needed them."

"Hannah will check on you regularly and make sure you get your medication," Ida Mae said.

"And you'll get Meals on Wheels, too," Reed added.

"The two of you are ganging up on me, are you?" Rose straightened in her seat. "You don't have to rough house me."

Ida Mae opened her mouth to protest, but then caught the gleam of humor in Rose's eye.

"I'd like to see the apartment," Rose went on. "And talk with Hannah a little bit. I do want my independence, and hate the idea of someone having to check on me, but I guess we're to the point where I'll have to give a little."

"I'll go over with you tomorrow morning," Ida Mae promised.

Heidi walked her to the door. "I feel so guilty," she said softly, glancing behind her. "What kind of person am I, kicking my husband's mother out into the street?"

"Hannah's apartment is a far cry from the street," Ida Mae said. "And she really is nice. So's her husband, but he's not home a lot, and when he is, he's asleep. You'll mostly be working with Hannah, if you need anything."

"Do you think this is the right thing to do?"

Ida Mae looked Heidi firmly in the eye. If there

was anything this woman needed, it was firmness and lots of it. "Heidi, your first priority is to your own children and husband. They need you right now, more than the ordinary family because of the challenges you've been given. If you try to spread yourself around, not only will it be too thin, but you're going to give yourself a nervous breakdown. I would not be suggesting this if I didn't think it would work."

She detected an internal sigh of relief in Heidi's features. "All right," she said, a smile appearing. "I think we'll go see the apartment."

Upon reaching her kitchen, Ida Mae called Hannah to set up a time. Ten o'clock was agreed upon, and then she asked after Joey. "Does he have a favorite treat or toy I could bring him tomorrow?"

"He really likes bubble gum," Hannah said.

"I'll bring some," Ida Mae promised.

After confirming with the Hunters, Ida Mae sat down and stared at the phone. She dared it to ring. Just let it try. Five whole minutes went by with no sound but the ticking of the hall clock. A miracle.

○—

Tansy and Ida Mae sat across from Anne Gimble, whose eyes were red from crying. "I just can't believe it," she said over and over. "My little girl is going to have a baby."

"When did you find out?" Ida Mae asked.

"Just a few days ago," Anne said. "I'm still in shock."

"She's seventeen, is that right?" Tansy asked.

"She just turned eighteen. I guess she's an adult now, like that makes any difference." She sniffed and dabbed at her nose with the tissue balled up in her hand.

Ida Mae ignored the bitter tone in Anne's voice, knowing she spoke out of fear. "Darcy's a good girl, Anne. The two of you will find a way to make it through this."

"A good girl? Sister Babbitt, she's pregnant."

"I know she is, Anne. But she's got a good heart."

"How is Darcy handling the news?" Tansy asked, intervening before Anne could reply to Ida Mae.

"She's really upset. She keeps telling me that she never meant for this to happen. But then, I don't know too many girls who get pregnant during their senior year and are happy about it. As for the father—what a laugh! He's just a boy himself. He can't be anyone's father." She shook her head and tried again. "The *father* was planning to put in his mission papers next month. It's just so sad."

"Is there anything we can do?" Tansy leaned forward and handed Anne a new tissue.

"I can't think of anything right now." Anne shook her head. "She can't be having a *baby*."

"It does seem impossible," Ida Mae agreed. She was in a unique situation, one of being able to empathize from personal experience. She didn't want to say anything, but she knew Anne needed to hear what she was going to say.

"About thirty years ago, I was in the same situation you're in, Anne," she said, choosing her words carefully as though picking her way through a minefield. "My daughter came to me and told me she was pregnant. She gave the baby up for adoption. It was a really rough time for our family because she didn't understand the consequences of what she'd done, and her lifestyle just kept getting more wild. Darcy's a good girl, Anne. She won't have to go through the years of heartache my daughter has. She's going to be just fine."

"I just can't help but feel like she's ruined," Anne said. "What kind of future can she have now? What decent man is going to want her?"

Ida Mae stiffened. *Be calm,* she said to herself. *You are here on the Lord's errand.* "We've been given the ability to repent," she said as gently as she could.

Anne raised her shoulders. "Sure, she can repent and all that, but it's not really going to change anything. I mean, she'll still be pregnant."

"Of course she'll still be pregnant, Anne, but in the Lord's eyes, the sin will be gone. She will have the opportunity to find joy again. And when the baby comes, she'd be able to look at it and see it for what it is—a precious manifestation of a miracle, and not the evidence of sin."

"But what about getting married someday? Will she be able to find someone who wants to marry a girl who had a baby at her age?"

"She'll be able to find a man who believes in the power of the Atonement and who will love her for who she has become."

Anne grabbed another tissue. "What if she decides to keep the baby?"

"Then the Lord will help her raise it. Anne, the world has not come to an end. Darcy's life is just taking another turn. She knows she made a mistake. She wants to turn things around. Give her the chance to use this as a learning experience. I know Darcy, and I think she's going to make it through this."

Ida Mae finished her piece and sat back, emotionally exhausted. The mask of bitterness was still on Anne's face, and Ida Mae didn't know if anything she'd said had penetrated.

Tansy was closing up the visit now, with promises to check back in a few days. Ida Mae stood, only then realizing that her exhaustion was physical as well. Her knees nearly went out from under her, but she stubbornly forbade them to collapse. She made it out to the car, but sank into the seat, taking a deep breath.

"I didn't know about your daughter, Ida Mae," Tansy said as she buckled her seat belt.

"It was a bad time in our lives." Ida Mae shoved from her mind the memory of her husband yelling at their daughter, throwing abusive words in her face.

After dropping Tansy off, Ida Mae returned home to find a blue Honda parked in front of her house. The driver, a young woman, was still seated, but she got out when Ida Mae pulled into the driveway.

"Excuse me?" She approached, her high-heeled boots clicking on the concrete. Ida Mae had to fight a sharp stab of criticism. *Those boots will break her neck . . . but don't they make her legs look nice and long, and the belt matches perfectly, and so does her purse. Phew.*

"I'm looking for the Babbitts'. Is this the right place?"

"Yes, it is. I'm Ida Mae Babbitt."

"I'm Ashley Marshall. It's so nice to meet you."

Ashley offered a hand that was clad in black leather, which matched the boots and the purse and the belt. How cute and trendy. *Stop it, Ida Mae*, she thought firmly. "It's nice to meet you. What brings you to Omni?"

"I'm looking for Ren. I understand he's living with you."

Ah, she was looking for Ren. Very interesting. "Why don't you come in for a bit. Ren's not here, but he should be home soon."

"That would be nice. Thank you."

Ashley followed Ida Mae into the house and took the offered seat in the living room.

"Can I get you anything, Ashley? I've got all kinds of refreshments, sandwich makings, drinks."

"I'm fine, thank you. I'll just sit here and read this book, if you don't mind." She motioned toward Ida Mae's latest library find, and Ida Mae nodded.

"I'll just be starting dinner in the kitchen."

She was halfway through assembling her chicken enchiladas when she heard Ren call out. He came in through the garage and kitchen door, bypassing the living room.

"Aunt Ida Mae, I think I've figured out the gadget we need out at the Dunns'. It'll be a motion sensor, and—"

"Hello, Ren." Ashley stood in the kitchen doorway, rather rudely interrupting Ren's sentence. Ida Mae didn't know why she couldn't let Ren explain his new invention. It sounded fascinating.

"Ashley."

Ida Mae glanced back and forth. Ashley looked pensive, Ren looked stoic, and she realized she'd better leave the room.

"I'll go check my e-mail," she said, knowing her excuse sounded stupid, but also knowing they weren't listening to her anyway.

She went into the guest room and sat down at the computer chair. She closed the door behind her, but Ren and Ashley were speaking loudly enough, she heard every word. It wasn't eavesdropping if they didn't care, was it?

"So, how have you been, Ren?"

"Just fine. And you?"

"Fine."

A long pause.

"What brings you to Omni?"

"You."

There was a bold statement. Ida Mae would never have said something like that when she was a young lady. Times were changing, that was for sure.

"I don't understand, Ashley. What do you want?"

"I miss you, Ren. I want you to come back."

Ida Mae leaned forward. This was a new development.

"I can't do that. You know I can't."

Ashley's sigh of exasperation was loud enough to be heard plainly, closed door or not. "But why? Why can't you?"

"I'm not the man you want, Ashley. You want someone who is ready to step into your father's shoes at his company, run things like he would. I can't do that. I don't *want* to do that."

"But you love me, don't you, Ren?"

"I did, very much. But I think you were in love with the *idea* of me, but not who I really am."

"So that's it, then. You're going to let me walk out the door." Ida Mae couldn't see Ashley's face, but she'd bet there was a pout involved.

"If you're ready to love me for who I am, then I'll come with you. But if you still want me to be someone different, I'll stay right here."

Ida Mae silently applauded.

"Is it so wrong to want you to be successful? Why is that bad?"

"I *am* successful. I have enough money, I'm happy, and I have a family who loves me. I don't know what else you want."

"All right, then. But don't come crawling back to me when you change your mind." Ashley's tone went from wheedling to hard as nails in two seconds flat.

"I won't."

Won't come crawling, or won't change his mind? Ida Mae wondered.

She listened to the tap-tap-tapping of Ashley's heels cross the floor and step over the threshold before she came out of the room. She was anxious to check on Ren. He had sounded so calm during his talk with Ashley, but she wanted to know how he was really feeling.

He sat at the kitchen table, staring into space.

"Ren? Are you all right?"

He turned his head and met her eye. "I'm fine, Auntie. I'm just tired of the whole dating game, you know? A girl gets you in her sights and starts wanting to change you. Sometimes it's little things, sometimes it's big things, but they all want you to be someone else. Why can't anyone just appreciate who you are?"

"I don't know, dear. But I think you're pretty wonderful."

"Now I need to find someone just like you," he said, standing up. "Can I help with dinner?"

"You can set the table, please."

They worked together in companionable silence until the meal was ready.

"Why would I want to get back with Ashley when I've got you?" Ren raised his water glass in a toast. "To Aunt Ida Mae. May her cheese grater never fail."

Chapter 14

"Thank goodness you're all here," Ida Mae told her counselors after dinner. "Ren's been home for an hour, and he won't tell me anything."

"Good for you, boy," Arlette said. "No fair spilling the beans without everyone here."

"My thoughts exactly," Ren said.

Ida Mae wasn't sure she liked the idea of Ren and Arlette ganging up on her. "Now, on to business," she said. "Ren, the floor is yours."

"I have two things to report," he said. "First, I followed Nick today. He left his house and drove into Salt Lake, stopping at the McDonald's on the outskirts of town. He ordered, I believe, a breakfast muffin."

"I bet it had meat on it," Arlette said.

"I bet it did too," Ren said. "After McDonald's, he drove to a warehouse a few blocks away. He spent the day driving a forklift in and out of the building. Sometimes it had pallets on it, and sometimes not. It looked like a pretty normal work day, to me. He took a break around noon and ate from a lunch pail in his truck. Then he drove the fork lift until around four this afternoon. From what I could tell by glancing through the bay doors, he then worked for half an hour in the shipping department, putting containers in cardboard boxes and covering them with packing peanuts. He came home by way of the grocery store. I stayed in the car, but it looked like he bought milk."

"That's so . . . unsuspicious," Tansy said, disappointment on her face.

"Yeah, that's what I thought, too. But there's more."

Tansy immediately perked up. "What?"

"Most of the cars in the employee lot were trucks or economy vehicles. All except for one."

"A black Jaguar," Arlette inserted.

Ren threw her an admiring glance. "That's right. There was a black Jaguar parked right by the loading dock."

"Could you tell if it was the same car?" Ida Mae asked.

"There weren't any distinguishing marks on it, so I can't say for sure. But I did get the license plate number."

"It didn't have mud on the plates?" Tansy asked.

"No, but that doesn't mean it's not the same one. He could easily have taken it through a car wash."

They all sat in silence for a minute, Ida Mae transcribing the new information onto her chart.

"I don't suppose any of you have a friend who works for the DMV?" she asked. Everyone shook their heads.

"I did a big favor for the DMV when I got my Earl to stop driving," Tansy said. "They sent me a Christmas ham that year."

"Ren, who owns the warehouse?" Ida Mae asked.

"It belongs to the Baby Mine company."

Ida Mae jotted that down. "So, what does this mean?" she asked, looking up. "Nick is working at a warehouse. There's nothing wrong with that."

"If the black Jaguar belongs to someone at work, why did that person drive all the way out here?" Arlette asked. "Why not just talk to Nick at work?"

"Excellent question." Ida Mae wrote it down and circled it. "Unless it's a coincidence and we're dealing with two cars."

"But how many people can say they know *two* people who own black Jags?" Ren asked. "I don't even know one, and I used to live in San Francisco, where there are a lot more cars to be had."

"Good point." Ida Mae wrote it down as well.

"Now, here's the thing," Ren said, leaning forward. "There's a help wanted sign in the window. I asked in the office—don't worry, Nick didn't see me—and they said they need a clerk."

Tansy tapped a finger on her lips. "What we need is someone to infiltrate the warehouse," she said. "An inside man." She cast her eyes over at Ren.

"It can't be Ren," Ida Mae objected.

"Why not, Auntie?" Ren asked. "Surely in today's modern world, a man can be anything he wants to be."

"Sooner or later, Nick would find out that Ren's from Omni," Ida Mae explained. "If he's doing something shady, he's not going to want anyone from home that close to his situation."

"And it certainly can't be me," Arlette said, with the air of someone who is being begged but must, regrettably, say no. "The last time I tried to type, it was on one of those horrid manual things, and I nearly broke my pinkie finger trying to hit the *a*. I'm under doctor's orders never to type again."

"I can type thirty words a minute," Tansy said hopefully, but Ida Mae shook her head.

"We're all too old, ladies. I hate to admit such a nasty thing, but it's true."

"I've got an idea, but I need to make a phone call first," Arlette said. "Let me get back to you tomorrow."

"All right." Ida Mae made another note on her pad. "Now, Ren, you said you had two things to report."

He sat up a little straighter. "Indeed, I do. I do, indeed." He reached into his pocket and pulled out a mass of wires. "This is my new invention."

Tansy clasped her hands together. Arlette scowled. Ida Mae asked, "What is it?"

"A motion detector. We'll string it across the trees there by the Dunns' shed, and it will record any movement that takes place."

"Any movement? What about birds and things like that?" Arlette asks.

"I thought about that myself, but I've worked out the bugs, I think. It will record movement that is slower than twenty miles an hour. If a car pulls back there, it has to go about fifteen to make it around the potholes. This will help us figure out when the Jaguar comes and goes."

"I think it's too risky," Arlette said. "Anything could trip it."

"That's why I attached the second part," Ren added. "This is a camera that is activated by the motion sensor. When the sensor is tripped, the camera snaps a picture. And it has a timestamp feature on it."

Arlette gave a grudging nod. "Very good."

"I don't know when I can go set it up. I've got to work tomorrow and I'm just beat after today. But we'll get it up there in the next day or two."

The group broke up and the ladies made their way to the door. "What is this phone call you're going to make, Arlette?" Ida Mae asked.

"I'd rather not say until I know for sure it will work," Arlette said. "I'll call you soon."

Ida Mae double-locked the door behind her presidency and turned, leaning against the jamb. She was so tired, she could hardly stand up.

"Ren," she called out. "I'm going to bed."

He appeared immediately. "Are you all right, Auntie?"

"I'm fine, dear. It's just been a long day."

Bed had never looked so good. Ida Mae brushed her teeth, pulled on her robe, and expected to be asleep before she even got the covers pulled up, but she couldn't stop thinking about the DMV.

Chapter 15

Hannah met Ida Mae and the Hunters at the front door, holding it wide open for them to pass inside.

"I brought Joey some gum and coloring books," Ida Mae told Hannah, passing over a bag.

"Thank you. I know he'll be so glad to get them."

Ned sat with the boys while Hannah took the Hunters and Ida Mae to see the apartment. Rose expressed her approval of the yellow and forest green décor, the daisy curtains in the kitchen, and the spacious bedroom.

"I think this will work for me, if you don't mind having me down here," she said to Hannah. "I don't want to be a bother."

"You'd be no bother," Hannah assured her. "We'd love to have you."

"That's what everyone says, until they've actually had me around for a little while." Rose winked.

"Let's go back upstairs and take care of the rental agreement," Hannah said, leading the way. When they walked into the Eyres' kitchen, Rose spoke up.

"Can I see your little boy for a minute?"

"Sure." She led Rose to the back while Ida Mae pulled out chairs for Reed and Heidi.

"The apartment is very cute," Heidi said. "I think Mother Hunter will be happy here."

"I think so too," Reed said, the first opinion he'd shared all morning.

"The boy is a darling," Rose said, reentering the room. "And I wouldn't worry. He should be out of pain soon. It's just a natural part of healing."

"Mother was a nurse for several years," Reed explained.

"Are you sure the children won't be too loud for you?" Hannah asked.

"They'll be just fine, dear. I raised children myself and know how they are."

The papers were signed, and the Hunters went home after arranging to move Rose in the following week. Ida Mae stayed behind to talk to Hannah and Ned for a minute.

"Thank you for arranging this, Sister Babbitt," Ned

said, bouncing Jeremiah on his knee. "I don't mean to sound greedy, but that extra money will really help us out."

"I'm glad I was able to help. And if it gets to be too much work, just let Reed know, and he'll find her another place to stay."

"I can't predict the future, but I think we'll get along just fine," Hannah said.

○—

"I don't see why I have to be the decoy," Arlette said. "Do I look like a duck to you?"

"You have a special role to play," Ida Mae told her. "We can use your natural grumpiness."

"Natural grumpiness? Is that a compliment?"

"It will be an asset to us today."

The Secret Sisters, plus Ren, sat in Arlette's minivan outside the Omni Department of Motor Vehicles. Ida Mae knew that only one employee was inside at a time—the city simply couldn't afford more, and to be honest, there wasn't a need for more. The office was only open one day a week.

"Who's working today?" Tansy asked.

They had a fifty-fifty guess on that one, with only two employees on staff. It would either be Bertha or

Donna, and they would both suit the purpose. Ida Mae leaned forward and squinted, trying to see through the window. After a moment, she caught a glimpse of a blonde beehive. "It's Donna," she said.

"Well, we might as well get this over with." Arlette opened the driver's door and slung her bag over her shoulder.

"Break a leg!" Tansy called out.

Arlette entered the double glass doors, a determined set to her shoulders. Ida Mae and the others counted to a hundred, then got out of the van. Ren led the way as they approached the building, and peered inside the door.

"She's in the back," he said, opening the door the remainder of the way. Ida Mae entered, with Ren close behind. Tansy stayed outside on the sidewalk, standing guard.

Ida Mae could hear Arlette's voice from the back room where the camera was kept.

"I just don't like the way I look in this picture," she said. "Can you take a new one?"

"All right, Arlette," came Donna's voice.

Ida Mae knew it would take Donna at least two minutes to remind herself how the camera worked. She gave Ren a thumbs-up, and he slunk over to the computer.

"Arlette, did I tell you about my new grandbaby?" Donna's voice had a strident quality to it that in the past had always driven Ida Mae just a little insane, but today she counted it a blessing. She would be able to tell exactly where they were in the picture-taking process as long as Donna kept talking.

Ren tapped something on the keyboard, then grunted. "There's a password," he whispered.

"It's got to be something simple," Ida Mae whispered back. "Donna isn't terribly deep." A flash of guilt made her wonder if she really should have said that, but it was too late now. She'd have to add it to her list of "things to repent for" later, and somehow she figured that trying to hack into the DMV computer was a little more serious than calling someone a name.

"There we are!" Donna proclaimed. "You look lovely."

"No, I don't," Arlette replied. "This piece of hair is sticking up."

"Well, there's a mirror. Why don't you fix it and then we can take another shot."

Ren stuck his tongue out the corner of his mouth, just like he used to do when he was a little boy and couldn't get his shoelaces to tie.

"Anything?" she asked.

"No."

Just then, Tansy started to cough, the pre-arranged signal that someone was coming. Ida Mae darted behind the counter with Ren and they both ducked. Around the edge of the counter, Ida Mae could see the sheriff walk past the building, his belt bulging with handcuffs, a nightstick, and the evidence of too many donuts. She didn't know whose idea it had been to make the entire front of the building a series of windows, but it wasn't helping her cause any.

After Ricky passed, she and Ren stood back up.

"Are you ready?" Donna asked.

"Yes."

"Now, let's see here." Another two minutes for Donna to use the camera. They'd bought some time, but not much.

"Try her birthday," Ida Mae whispered.

"I don't know her birthday," Ren said.

"April 29th."

Ren turned to her with surprise on his face. "How on earth did you know that?"

"I'm the Relief Society president. I know everything."

Ren keyed in the date, but it didn't work. He tried month and day, then 4-29, and 4-2-9. No matter what he did, the screen wouldn't change.

"Now I look like a plucked hen," Arlette said. "Maybe I could pose a little differently, like a three-quarter profile or something."

"They really want a shot from the front," Donna explained. "They want to be able to see as much of you as possible."

"If I get pulled over, I could pose the same way I am in the picture," Arlette suggested.

"I don't think that's a good idea. Let's try one more," Donna said.

Tansy coughed, and Ida Mae and Ren dropped.

"Oh, no," Ida Mae whispered. "It's Bertha, and she's coming in." She wanted to bury her face in her hands, but like Utah drivers passing the scene of an accident, she had to stare.

Tansy greeted Bertha cheerfully, waving her arms around like some caffeinated mime. Bertha smiled and pulled out her wallet, showing Tansy what could only be pictures of her grandchildren.

"Smart girl," Ida Mae murmured, wondering why she never seemed to give Tansy enough credit. That maneuver alone would keep Bertha tied up for at least five minutes.

Ren rose halfway, just enough to reach the keyboard, and kept entering whatever words Ida Mae could think of.

"I'm sorry, Arlette, but sometimes that camera just won't spit out a decent picture," Donna said, and Ida Mae realized her voice was coming from the hall, not the back room. She grabbed Ren's collar and yanked him down just as Donna entered the room, talking over her shoulder to Arlette. "We could try all afternoon and still not be happy with the results. But think of it this way—no one really likes their driver's license picture, do they?"

"But that's them. I'm talking about me," Arlette explained.

Ida Mae crawled forward two feet and caught Arlette's eye as she entered the room. Arlette blinked, then nodded.

"Tell me about this ficus tree in the corner," she said, taking Donna's elbow and steering her away from the counter.

Ren and Ida Mae began to crawl, inching their way out from behind the counter and toward the door.

"Well, it's just plastic, really. We got it at Walmart."

"I don't remember seeing it the last time I was here," Arlette said.

"We only got it last month, I think it was. Or maybe the month before . . . it was right after Heathcliff Jones renewed his license. I remember that because he told us our office looked a little drab, and he suggested a plant. Bertha and I headed right down that very night and got this ficus."

Ida Mae wasn't making very much progress. Ren was already at the door and glanced back over his shoulder at her, raising his eyebrows, but she was already doing the best she could. Her knees just couldn't take this kind of pressure. For a second, she wondered about reversing course and trying to get back to the counter, but Bertha was starting to turn.

Everything went into slow motion.

Bertha turned.

Tansy grabbed her elbow and said something with a great deal of animation, hanging on for dear life.

Ren made it the rest of the way to the door and slipped out, coming to his feet as he did so.

Ida Mae inched another foot, clearing the counter area and yet not quite making it to the door.

Donna turned and took a step toward the counter . . . and saw Ida Mae.

"Why, Ida Mae! What on earth are you doing on the floor?"

There comes a time in every woman's life when she's asked a question that could possibly incriminate her. For some, it's, "Does this make me look fat?" or "Do you think Ralph is cheating on me?" For others, it's, "Did you eat the last brownie?" Ida Mae wished for one of those questions. She'd be more than happy to say, "You look wonderful, Ralph loves you, and yes, I did eat the brownie, but I'll make another pan." Instead, she mustered up her courage and every acting skill she'd learned from Ginger Rogers over the years and said, "I dropped a contact lens."

Donna was at her side in a flash, which was funny, considering she'd just taken several pictures. Ida Mae knew she had to get a grip on herself, and soon, or she'd start into a high-blown fit of hysterical laughter that would probably last until well after they got her safely buckled into her straight jacket. Arlette joined them, and they dutifully scoured every inch of the floor looking for the lens.

"I must have lost it at home or in the car," Ida Mae said at last, coming to her feet.

"I didn't know you wore contact lenses," Donna said, scooting the chairs back from their pulled-out-to-be-looked-under positions.

"That's right!" Ida Mae brought her hands to her cheeks. "I don't!"

She ducked out of the building as fast as she could, wanting to put as much distance as possible between the newly befuddled Donna and herself. Tansy let go of Bertha's arm, Ren joined them around the corner of the building, and Arlette came a moment later. They collapsed in the van, all breathing heavily.

"How'd it go?" Tansy asked after several long seconds.

"We weren't able to get into the computer," Ida Mae said. "There was a password."

"Edgar," Tansy said.

"What?" Ren turned and looked at her.

"Bertha told me. The password on the computer is Edgar. It's the name of Donna's new baby grandson."

"Did you ask, or did she tell you that?" Arlette asked.

"She just told me. Really, someone ought to explain to her how dangerous that is."

All went quiet for a moment while they processed the information.

"Should we go back in?" Ren asked.

"Not on your life!" Arlette replied. "That was worse than almost anything I've ever experienced."

Ida Mae didn't say anything, but internally, she'd never agreed with Arlette more.

Arlette put the keys in the ignition and started the engine. They were halfway home before Ren voiced what Ida Mae was sure they'd all been thinking.

"Who names a baby Edgar?"

○—

The phone rang at seven thirty the next morning—an irritating wake-up call right by Ida Mae's head.

"County morgue," she mumbled into the receiver. "Which dead person do you want to talk to?"

Arlette ignored her. "My granddaughter has come to stay with me for a few weeks. I told her what we're doing with the Dunns. She thinks it's despicable and wants to help."

Ida Mae blinked. "She thinks it's despicable, but she still wants to help?"

"Yes."

"Okay," she said. "Bring her around this afternoon, and we'll fill her in. Was this your surprise?"

"Yes. When we decided we needed someone to work at the warehouse, she was the first person to come to mind."

"Sounds good. Bring her over around three, okay?"

"Okay."

Ida Mae checked her calendar, amazed to see there was nothing written on it. Everything she'd been doing lately had come up so fast, she hadn't had time to write it down. She'd only had time to fly out the door and react.

She ran a load of dishes and folded some laundry, feeling blessed to have the time. In days past, she wouldn't do a single other thing until all her housework was done, but she hadn't had that luxury in years. Truth be told, she sort of liked putting off her work until later. It made her feel just a tiny bit rebellious.

The doorbell rang smack on the nose of three. She opened the door to find Tansy, Arlette, and a pretty brunette girl standing on her porch.

"Come in," she said, hastening to unlatch the screen. "It's cold out there."

The women entered and pulled off coats and gloves, then settled down onto the living room couches. Ida Mae glanced at the clock, although she knew what time it was. Ren got off work at two thirty—she thought he'd be home by now.

"Ida Mae, this is my granddaughter, Eden," Arlette said, motioning with an orange-swathed knitting needle. "She's a detective."

"Well, not really," Eden said, her voice a little husky. Ida Mae thought she had a frog in her throat, but as the girl talked, Ida Mae realized it was her natural voice. She liked it—it wasn't too girly. "I'm actually a journalist who wants to write detective novels, but I love snooping out a good mystery in real life. Gives me a lot of material to use later."

"I just knew someone would want to write a book about us," Tansy said, a broad smile lighting her face.

"You haven't had any murders in this case, have you?" Eden asked.

"No, thank goodness," Ida Mae told her.

"Well, I'm mostly interested in murder stories, so I probably won't be writing this one. I'm sure someone will someday, though."

Tansy seemed somewhat mollified, although still disappointed.

The ladies spent the next few minutes bringing Eden up-to-date on everything that had happened. She seemed to appreciate the significance of the Wendy's wrapper, and that was a big load off Ida Mae's mind.

"Have you shared all this with the police?" Eden asked.

"We've tried talking to the police, but they say until we get some actual, concrete proof, they can't do anything to help us," Ida Mae told her. "They think we're just being silly."

"Nonsense," Eden said, studying the chart in front of her. "There's definitely something going on. You've got people acting out of character all over the place here. Mary, who is usually the best mother in the world, is worried about asking for assistance to keep her kids fed. Nick, who is usually a doting father and husband, is distant and withdrawn. Something's up."

"You got all that from this list?" Ida Mae asked. Maybe her charting skills weren't as hopeless as she thought.

"And from listening to everything you've said about the case," Eden said. "There's a lot of stuff you haven't written down. What are the people involved like? When they start behaving in an odd way, write that down too. It's all linked together."

"Smart girl," Tansy said approvingly, and Ida Mae nodded her agreement. Arlette was silent, but had a smug look on her face. Yes, Ida Mae had to admit, Arlette's idea had been a good one.

Ren came in a few minutes later, his arms full of bags and boxes. "Hey, Secret Sisters," he called out from the kitchen. "Sorry I'm late. I'll be there in a minute."

"My nephew," Ida Mae explained to Eden as Ren came around the corner, having dumped most of his load onto the kitchen table. His ponytail had come loose at some point, causing his hair to stick out at odd angles. He had a big smear of grease across his shirt, and he didn't look very respectable. Ida Mae nearly chastised herself for having the thought, but then stopped. This was an accurate assessment—she would allow it.

Eden looked him over with a bemused look on her face. "I'm told you're the nephew."

Ren stuck out his hand, noticed it wasn't clean, and withdrew it. "I haven't been told what you are yet."

"I'm Eden, Arlette's granddaughter. I understand I'm to apply for work at the warehouse. You know, be someone on the inside."

"You're going to help us?"

Ida Mae inwardly smiled at the surprised look on Ren's face. It took a lot to ruffle the boy, but now, if he were any more ruffled, he'd be a potato chip.

"Is that all right with you?"

"Sure. I mean, if you want to."

"Oh, I do," Eden returned.

"Great. I say we call it, Operation Green Jell-O."

The two continued to size each other up good-naturedly, only calling an end to the verbal ping-pong when Tansy asked what was in all the bags Ren had brought home.

"Supplies," he supplied. "Wire, tape, hooks—all the stuff I'll need to make the trip wire and hang the camera from the tree."

"Cool," Eden said, coming to her feet. "Can I see?"

"Me too?" Tansy asked.

The group moved into the kitchen, where Ren spread out his plunder. "Some of this I got out at the scrap yard, and some I got at the hardware store," he explained. "I found the camera at a pawn shop."

"Very frugal," Arlette said approvingly. "Does it work?"

"Seems to." Ren went through each component, explaining the reasons for them.

"And this?" Eden asked, holding up a roll of duct tape.

"That is the magic that brings it all together. You can fix anything with duct tape, you know."

"So, what is the plan now?" Tansy asked.

"We need to get this camera into position. I think tonight would be best. Then tomorrow, Eden should go into the warehouse and see if she can get a job."

"I type eighty words a minute," Eden said, flicking her hair over her shoulder in a dramatic gesture. "What's not to hire?"

The group dispersed to their assignments. Ida Mae, Ren, and Eden would go out to the house that night and set up the camera. Tansy would go to the Eyres' house and stay the night so Hannah could sleep, and Arlette would do the same the following night.

"The McGuffey girls are coming over tomorrow to help Hannah with the boys while she cleans the apartment for Rose," Ida Mae reported, and everyone nodded. Hopefully everything was under control. Ida Mae tried to push her other worries to the back of her mind. Sufficient to the day are the tasks of the Relief Society, and she shouldn't worry about tomorrow while she was still working on today.

Chapter 16

Ren parked his car in the accustomed clearing, and Ida Mae pulled her black coat more closely around her. She had finally given in to the suggestion that they wear dark clothing. She did, however, draw the line at putting grease paint under her eyes. She didn't think the possible benefits were great enough to justify the mess.

Eden held Ren's tool bag, and he carried the camera equipment. Ida Mae was on hot chocolate duty, bringing up the rear with a large thermos. They moved slowly through the trees, able to pick out their path by the light of the half-moon reflected on the snow. Ida Mae had always loved the way it never really got dark in winter—the snow took on a luminescent quality that kept the darkness at bay.

The Dunns' shed loomed before them, and Ren held up his hand. They stopped walking as Ren crouched, pulling some wires out of his pocket. He glanced around, then motioned for Ida Mae to come closer.

"Duct tape," he whispered, and she reached into her fanny pack to retrieve it. She winced as she did so—who on earth had thought up the name "fanny pack?" What was wrong with something a little more appropriate, like, "waist purse" or "hand-free pouch" or "clip-on bag?" She handed over the tape, and he slid the roll onto his wrist like a bracelet.

Eden handed him a screwdriver, and he crept closer to the edge of the Dunns' property. Selecting a tree, he placed the camera on a branch, securing it with the tape. Then he screwed in some wires. Ida Mae wished she was a little more technologically savvy so she could understand what he was doing.

After he got the camera in place, he took some strips of brown cloth and used them to camouflage the slight shine of the tape.

"Good thinking," Eden whispered, and Ren smiled.

One of the long wires was brought down the length of the branch and stretched across to the outreaching limb of the next tree. Ren extended the wire three trees down from the camera and fastened it at every junction with the duct tape, fiddling with tools and gadgets and weird-looking gizmos all along the way. Ida Mae made herself useful by dispensing the hot chocolate after the first fifteen minutes had gone by— she couldn't feel her nose at all, it was so numb. Eden sipped gratefully as well, but Ren was in a groove and shouldn't be disturbed until the task was finished.

Which it finally was, after about a half hour. He took a cup and downed it.

"Test it out," he whispered to Eden.

"What should I do?"

"Go down there and walk slowly up the drive."

She disappeared, a little too completely for Ida Mae's taste. A few minutes later, she heard soft footsteps, and Eden reappeared like a shadow.

Ren looked at the camera. "Two pictures were taken," he verified. "Tomorrow we can double check the timestamp feature."

Ida Mae was so cold, she couldn't feel her thighs. As she climbed into the car, she rubbed her hands on her legs, trying to restore any sort of feeling.

"Sorry that took me so long," Ren said. "I wanted to be sure to get it just right."

"I thought it was exciting," Eden said. "Waiting to see if we'd get caught, concocting wild alibis, imagining how we'd flee through the trees to safety— I haven't had this much fun in a long time."

"You've got a strange idea of fun," Ida Mae said, even while she secretly agreed. She hadn't felt so alive since her twenties.

They drove home slowly, not taking the risk of speeding and getting pulled over by the sheriff or one of his men. They liked to patrol at odd hours of the night to keep the crime element down—or so the sheriff said. Ida Mae had to bite back a laugh at the thought. They had crime going on right here, and the sheriff didn't care.

○—

"I got the job," Eden announced, a grin spreading across her face. "I walked in, told them I was applying, and sat right down at the computer. He had me show him some basic skills, and I got hired on the spot."

"That's great," Ida Mae said. She handed the girl a cookie and a napkin. "Now we can start to investigate in earnest."

"We've been earnest," Tansy said, a wounded look crossing her face.

"We have, Tansy, and I didn't mean anything by it," Ida Mae soothed. She handed another cookie around that way as well, and all hurt feelings were mended.

"So, what's our plan for this week?" Arlette asked.

"Let's get Eden settled before we make that decision," Ida Mae said. "Ren is going to check the camera tonight and make sure the timestamp feature is working. Eden can report on the setup there at the warehouse, and once we hear from the two of them, we'll know what to do next."

Everyone in the room nodded.

"Now, when will Hannah be back with us?" Tansy asked.

"She's not sure, but I think we'll be okay without her for a little while. She's agreed to let me call her if I have any questions, and so far this morning, I've only had to call four times. That's progress, I believe." Ida Mae leaned forward and picked up the empty cookie plate. "I'll get a refill."

When she returned, she flipped through her agenda. "All right, now. Tansy, you checked in with the Sylvesters, right?"

"Yes, I did. Sister Sylvester is having a boy and two girls, isn't that wonderful? She's doing all right in bed, although she's still a bit bored. She's got books and movies, but she wants to be up and around, poor thing." All the women nodded.

"The bishop is feeling a little better, and his blood pressure went down again, just a mite. But things at work are getting hectic, so who knows how long that will last. I've got meals arranged for the rest of the week, and we're getting someone in to spell off the children's aunt on Friday night." Tansy sat back, beaming with pride in her report.

"Thank you, Tansy. A marvelous job as always. Arlette, how is the substitute teacher situation coming along?"

"I was able to get Sister Black and Sister Wilson to teach the last two Sundays of February," Arlette said. "Hopefully, the new teachers will be called soon."

"I submitted the names, but haven't wanted to pester the bishop about it," Ida Mae said.

"I understand," Arlette said, her knitting needles clicking righteously.

"Now, Eden, when do you start the new job?"

"Tomorrow."

"So soon? That's good," Ida Mae said. She thought for a moment, nodding. "If anything happens, you can go to a payphone on your break and let us know, all right? I'll jot down our numbers for you to call."

"Make sure Ren's cell number is on there," Arlette interjected. Her face went red, something Ida Mae had never seen before in all her days. "In case she needs backup, you know."

"I'll do that," Ida Mae promised.

The ladies streamed out, Eden remaining to help clean up. "I'm sorry to drag you in on all the Relief Society business," Ida Mae told her. "We try to keep our Secret Sisters meetings separate, but our duties overlap so much, we generally end up talking about everything all at once."

"That's all right," Eden said as she stooped to pick up a fallen napkin. "It was interesting. I always thought the Relief Society was a well-oiled machine—I didn't realize how much oil went into it."

"Quite a lot, and elbow grease, too. But it all gets spread around. I'll help one sister on Monday, and by Tuesday, she's out helping someone else."

"What about you, Ida Mae?" Eden fixed her with a discerning look. "Who takes care of you?"

Ida Mae blinked, taken aback. "I—well, I have Arlette and Tansy and Hannah, and I'm sure someone would come in and help me, if I needed anything."

"But you don't need anything? Not a single thing?"

Ida Mae thought for a minute. "Well, I did need one thing, and that was companionship. But Ren has taken care of that for me."

"About Ren," Eden asked slowly, moving toward another stray napkin. "Is he planning to be here long?"

"We haven't discussed a timeline, but I think he's happy here. He can stay as long as he likes, but of course, he's also free to go whenever he wants." Ida Mae looked at Eden, wondering what prompted this new line of questioning.

"And is he seeing anyone?"

Crystal clear focus shot into place. "He was, but he recently broke up with her. She wasn't his type." Ida Mae saw Eden's shoulders relax.

"I'm glad," Eden said. "Not that he had to break up, but that he knew it and fixed it. Too many people end up with boyfriends or girlfriends, or even spouses, that aren't good for them." A bitter tone crept into her voice, making Ida Mae curious about the history there.

"Did you have a bad breakup, dear?" she asked.

"No, I'm talking about my parents. They divorced when I was ten. I haven't had any bad breakups, because I've never let anyone get that close to me. I guess it's a throwback from all those childhood memories."

"I'm sorry. I didn't know." Ida Mae led the way into the kitchen, where she turned on the water and let the sink fill.

"I don't think Grandma talks about it much. She likes to focus on the positive."

Ida Mae coughed, reaching for a drink. After swallowing and making sure she wasn't about to have a lung come flying out, she said, as carefully as she could, "Has she always been so . . . positive?"

"My whole life. She told me, there's enough in the world to drag you down without looking for it. She's amazing, really. All those socks."

Ida Mae frowned, trying to understand the connection. "Socks?" she said at last, not being successful.

"The socks. You know, the socks she's always making. She donates them to the homeless shelter in Salt Lake."

"I didn't know that," Ida Mae said, pulling out a stool and sitting abruptly. "I just thought she liked to knit."

"She gets donations of yarn all through the year and spends her time making socks. Oh, but don't tell her I told you," Eden said quickly. "If she's been keeping it a secret, she'd be mad if I said anything."

"I won't say a word."

Ida Mae felt thoroughly foolish as she bid Eden goodbye and watched her drive away. All this time, she'd been so critical of Arlette's outrageous color choices, and she couldn't understand why she had to be knitting all the time, like she had some sort of wool compulsion. And now to find out that she was merely taking what she'd been given and turning it into something useful—something that would really benefit the recipient? Ida Mae shook her head. It was almost more than she could process.

Chapter 17

The Baby Mine Company manufactures formula, diapers, cribs, car seats—pretty much anything you can think of for a baby," Eden said. She pulled a brochure out from her bag. "This is a piece of literature they circulate to the stores. Baby food, clothing—it's all in there."

"I love their products," Hannah said, rejoining the meeting for the first time in a while. "Especially the diapers. They've got little blue bunnies on the outside, and they're really absorbent."

"Blue bunnies? Like Beatrix Potter?" Tansy asked.

"Sort of, but a little more cartoon-like. And the girl diapers have pink bunnies on them."

"Boy diapers and girl diapers?" Ren asked. "Does it really matter?"

"Some people think it does, but I'm not so sure," Hannah replied.

"Back to the matter at hand," Ida Mae spoke up. "Eden was just telling us about the warehouse."

"They ship their products all over the nation," Eden said. "Today I was given a tour of the facilities and the basic run-down of how everything works. The merchandise comes in from the factory and is stored in the warehouse. It's shipped out from there. One end of the building is the shipping area, and the rest is for storage. Nick's job is to unload the truck from the factory in the morning, and then in the afternoon to ship out the orders of baby food and formula. Other people are in charge of the orders for the larger items, like cribs and car seats."

Ida Mae scribbled furiously. "So he unloads the truck and then he packages product."

"Correct."

Ida Mae paused, nibbling on her pencil. "Ren says he saw the black Jaguar parked outside the warehouse the other day. Was it there today?"

"Yes, it was. The man in the Jaguar is James Jeffries. He's the vice president of the company, thirty-five years old, single, has dark hair and eyes, a small moustache, likes French cuisine, and stands about six feet tall."

Ida Mae blinked. That was a lot more information

than she'd expected for just one day on the job, and certainly more than they ever would have been able to glean from the DMV computer, if they'd been successful—which they hadn't. But she was choosing not to dwell on that.

"How did you learn all that?" Arlette asked. "I thought you were going to be surreptitious."

"I was," Eden said. "But after watching the Jaguar all day, and not seeing anyone go near it, I decided to take matters into my own hands. I went up to Nichole, one of the other female employees, asked her who owned the Jaguar, and if he was single."

"And you got all that information?" Ren asked.

"Of course," Eden said, flapping one hand in his direction. "Women love to talk about men."

"I've also heard that women can smell fear," he replied. "Is that true?"

"Of course," she said again.

Ida Mae decided to intervene before the conversation got any more . . . interesting. She turned to Ren. "Do you have anything to report?"

"I went out to the Dunns' early this morning to check the camera. The Jag came by at eight o'clock last night."

"Could you see if the driver delivered another envelope?"

177

"The camera doesn't have that wide an angle. We've got it set to cover the driveway, not clear up by the shed."

"Eight o'clock," Ida Mae murmured, jotting down the time. "Okay, let's get back to Nick's job. It sounds perfectly respectable to me."

"There has to be something we're missing," Arlette said. "There's nothing sinister about baby food."

"I don't know about that," Hannah said. "Have you ever tasted the veal?"

○—

Days went by with nothing to report. Eden enjoyed her job, not just the spying but the actual clerking as well. James Jeffries apparently liked to keep to the shadows—Arlette's theory that evil loves darkness possibly being proven—because Eden hadn't actually seen him at work, even though the car was there. Ren checked the camera at the Dunns' four days a week, and the ladies were able to establish a pattern—the Jaguar showed up every ten days, around eight o'clock at night.

Rose had settled well in Hannah's basement, Heidi was learning how to communicate with her son through sign language, and Joey would be getting his cast off in a few short days. Everything seemed to be humming along as usual. Ida Mae checked her to-do list and noticed that everything was blissfully calm. It was boring.

The monotony ended one afternoon when the phone rang. "It's Eden. Can I meet with all of you tonight?"

"Certainly," Ida Mae said, making a note in her appointment book. As she hung up the phone, she noticed her heart was starting to thump a little faster. She had something to look forward to.

She spent the rest of the day cleaning her house, keeping one eye on the clock. When seven o'clock hit, she grew anxious. Where were the others? Had something happened to them?

She threw the door wide when she heard the first footsteps on the porch. "Come in," she said, taking Eden's coat, then Arlette's. "Ren's in his room, and Tansy will be here any minute."

Once everyone was seated, Eden got straight to the point. "Nick came into the office today," she said. "He needed the zip code for Tulsa. I looked it up for him."

"I'm not sure why that's significant," Ida Mae said.

"Whenever an order comes in, the address is printed right on the order form," Eden explained. "For some reason, that order didn't have a complete address.

I took the form and looked it over. It appeared to be normal, except for the missing zip code. And the fact that I didn't print it out."

Ida Mae's confusion must have shown on her face.

Eden explained. "It's my job to take the orders and create shipping labels for them," she said. "I can do that basically by clicking 'print' in the right software, but we're required to put our initials down in the bottom of the form. I click on a box, up comes a text field, I input my initials, click save, and then print. My initials are on the bottom of every form I print. I double check as they come out of the printer. It's a precaution on the part of the company—if an order gets goofed up, they know who to blame. The person who ships the package also initials the form so we know who packed the box."

"So, let me get this straight," Ren said. "Every order form you send down to the shipping area has your initials on it."

"That's right. And I'm the only person in the company who processes orders. The other secretary answers the phones, makes out the paychecks, and all that. She doesn't do orders."

"So, this order comes through with no zip code, Nick brings it to you, and you see that it doesn't have your initials," Ren continued.

"That's right. Besides, I can't process an order without an entire address. If I don't have the full address, I have to call the customer up and get it before we process it."

"You're saying someone slipped an order form into the stack without your knowledge," Ida Mae said.

"That's exactly what I'm saying. Someone used the company form and printed out the order, but it didn't come through my desk."

Ren leaned back, looking thoughtful. "What was the order for?"

"A case of baby formula."

"Soy or milk based?" Tansy asked.

"Milk based," Eden said.

"My boys never could drink milk," Arlette said. "I think lactose intolerance runs in my family."

The room fell quiet as everyone thought over what they'd learned. "Eden," Ida Mae said after a while, "you must have access to the company's computer database for orders, right? I mean, you can go back and see what's been ordered in the last few days."

"Yes, I can."

"Why don't you see what you can find out about this order? Maybe whoever placed it left some kind of telltale information on it."

"Good thinking, Auntie," Ren said. "Maybe there will be a timestamp or something on it."

"I'll do it first thing," Eden said. "I'm swamped in the morning with all the Internet orders that come in late at night—I'll squeeze it in the middle of that and no one will be the wiser."

The group chatted for another few minutes, then rose and prepared to leave. The phone rang just as Ida Mae was encouraging Tansy to take some cookies home to Earl.

"It's Anne Gimble," said a woman's shaky voice on the other end. "Darcy's missing."

Chapter 18

Ren drove Eden home while Arlette, Tansy and Ida Mae made their way to the Gimbles' house. Anne met them on the front porch, her eyes red from crying.

"The police say they can't classify her as a missing person yet, because we haven't been able to reach all her friends," she told them. "And she's too old for an Amber Alert, and we don't know that she's been kidnapped. I just want them to do something right now—I can't take this waiting."

"When did you notice she was gone?" Ida Mae asked.

"She didn't come home from school, and I thought she must have gone home with Tracey. She does that sometimes—Tracey's the only one who knows she's pregnant, so she spends a lot of time there. But then I got an automated call from the high school, saying she'd missed all her classes. I called Tracey's house to talk to Darcy about skipping school, and Tracey said she hadn't seen Darcy today at all."

"Does she take the bus to school?" Arlette asked.

"She rides with friends, or she drives. They take turns carpooling."

Ida Mae motioned toward the house. "Let's go inside, Anne. It's getting cold out here."

"I'm sorry—I wasn't thinking. Please, come in."

The ladies redistributed themselves in the Gimbles' living room. "The police say they'll send some cars around tonight to see what they can find, and tomorrow, if she hasn't shown up, they'll launch a full-scale investigation," Anne said. "I know she's old enough to take care of herself, but she's still my baby, you know?"

"We do know," Tansy said, patting Anne's hand.

The phone rang a moment later, and Anne jumped for it. "Hello?" she said. "Is that you, Darcy?"

She listened for a moment and her face fell. "No. Really?" She pressed her fingertips to her forehead. "Me either. Well, okay, and you do the same."

She resumed her seat. "That was Grant Markham, Paul's father. Paul is Darcy's boyfriend. Apparently, he's missing too."

Ida Mae opened her eyes. She'd only meant to close them for a minute, but now sunlight streamed into the Gimbles' living room and she had a crook in her neck from slumping down in the sofa. A glance around told her that Arlette and Tansy were in much the same state. Anne stood at the window, her fist clenching a panel of curtain.

"I'm sorry," she said without turning. "I shouldn't have kept you so late. It was selfish of me."

"You needed us here," Ida Mae said, remembering Anne's violent sobs of the night before after receiving the Markham's phone call. "It wasn't selfish at all."

"I'd hoped she was over at his house," Anne said. "At least then I'd know where she was."

Arlette and Tansy began to stir at the sound of voices. "What time is it?" Arlette asked.

"It's seven o'clock," Anne told her.

"I have to say, for an antique, this couch is pretty comfortable," Arlette said, coming to her feet. She stretched, reminding Ida Mae of a cat. "I don't suppose there's been any word?"

"No, not yet," Anne said.

"Has anyone told the sheriff that the children are probably together?" Tansy asked.

"Grant Markham said he'd call them right after he got off the phone with me." Anne turned from the window. "I owe you ladies a nice breakfast."

"Oh, we couldn't put you out," Tansy said, but Anne held up a hand.

"I insist. And you haven't lived until you've tasted my waffles."

The front door opened and Bob Gimble stepped into the house, his overcoat askew and his hair rumpled. He looked just like *Columbo.*

"Anything?" Anne asked, and Bob shook his head.

"I went to her friends' houses, to all the spots where I know she likes to go. I even drove into Salt Lake and Provo and went to some of the places she's mentioned in the past. Most of them were closed, and she wasn't hanging around outside. But it's so cold out there, I didn't really expect to find her outside anyway."

"I'm about to make breakfast," Anne said. "Come in by the heater where it's warm."

Bob took off his coat and seemed to notice the ladies for the first time. "Good morning," he said, nodding.

"Were you out all night, Bob?" Tansy asked.

"Ever since I found out," he said.

They gathered around the table and sipped orange juice until Anne set a steaming platter of waffles down in front of them, complete with three different flavors of syrup. Ida Mae had to admit, the waffles were even better than her own.

"You need to eat something, Anne," Tansy said, motioning toward Anne's untouched plate. "What good will you be to Darcy if you get sick?"

Anne mechanically cut a couple of squares from her waffle and shoved them in her mouth. She had just swallowed when the doorbell rang, and she jumped, dropping her fork.

"I'll get it," she and Bob both said, but Bob beat her to the door by a couple of feet. They opened the door standing side by side.

Sheriff Ricky Shelton stood on the porch, his hat in his hands.

"It's not what you think," he said before Bob or Anne could ask the question. "She's alive and fine. But let's sit down and talk."

Anne led the way into the living room. Ida Mae, Tansy, and Arlette stayed in the dining room, but they could still hear every word.

"Now, Bob, Anne, just let me assure you that Darcy is fine," Ricky said again. "You may not like what I have to say, but let's keep everything in perspective."

"You're leading up to something," Bob said. "Please, just tell us what it is."

"Darcy and Paul drove in to Salt Lake yesterday morning, bought bus tickets, and went down to Las Vegas. They arrived there around ten o'clock last night, found an all-night wedding chapel, and were married."

"But, she's just a child," Anne said, her voice strangled.

"You told me she turned eighteen a short time ago," Ricky said. "She's legally old enough to get married."

Ida Mae heard the shifting of a chair. She wished she could see facial expressions, but even she had limits when it came to spying, so she stayed put.

"So, they're in Las Vegas," Bob reiterated.

"That's right."

"Thanks for looking into it, Ricky."

"Not a problem. I wasn't going to start the investigation until a little later today, but I needed to go to the bus station anyway and thought I'd ask. It all came out from there."

"What was the name of the wedding chapel?" Anne asked.

Ida Mae heard the rustling of paper. "Maxie's Heavenly Chapel on the Strip."

"That's horrid."

"Yes, it certainly is." Ida Mae heard the paper rustle again, and the sheriff continued. "Best thing you folks can do now is to wait for Darcy to call. She's an adult, she's a married woman now, and it's up to her to make the next move."

A few minutes later, Bob and Anne rejoined the ladies in the dining room. "I guess you heard," Anne said.

"We did," Ida Mae told her.

"But if you want us to pretend we didn't, we can do that, too," Tansy added.

"Ricky's right, Anne. Be grateful Darcy's safe," Arlette said.

"Maxie's Heavenly Chapel on the Strip," Anne said, pushing her waffle around on her plate. "That's sure a far cry from the temple."

"But you know what—I bet they'll head for the temple on their first anniversary," Tansy said. "They're good kids, Anne. They made a mistake, but this isn't the end."

"I know a lot of kids who've gotten married civilly and then were sealed later," Bob added. "If I know Darcy, and I believe I do, she's trying to make things right. She'll come around."

"I wish she'd call," Anne said.

Ida Mae rose. "Anne, now that Bob's home, I think we'll get going. You've got a lot to discuss, and I'm sure you both want a long nap."

"Thank you for coming, Ida Mae, ladies. I never meant for you to spend the night on my couch."

"Don't think anything of it."

Chapter 19

The next day was Sunday, and Ida Mae was having a hard time concentrating on her duties. Eden wouldn't be able to check the computer until Monday morning, and couldn't report until Monday night, so there was no news on that front. What really distressed Ida Mae was the fact that she kept catching whispers about Darcy in the hallway, and she hated the idea that the sisters in her ward were gossiping. Anne was nowhere to be seen during sacrament meeting, and Ida Mae figured she was lying low. But as the prelude music came to an end in Relief Society, she saw Anne slip in and take a seat halfway up on the left.

"Welcome to Relief Society, sisters," Ida Mae said, smoothing down her skirt. "I have a few brief announcements. Lacey Duvall had her baby, a little girl. They're both home and doing well, but we have a sign-up sheet for meals going around." She glanced at Anne, who seemed to be holding herself together well. *So far, so good.*

"Next Wednesday is our excursion to the temple. We're meeting at Sister Browning's house at five thirty to carpool."

"In the morning?" asked a shocked voice in the back of the room.

"No, in the evening."

The sigh of relief would have started a hurricane if properly channeled.

"Now it's time for our Good News Minute. Does anyone have some good news?"

Anne's hand flew up in the air. Ida Mae felt her eyebrows go up just about as fast, but she nodded. "Anne?"

"I got a call from Darcy this morning. She got married on Friday night, and they're going to be looking for an apartment in Springville, where her new husband just got a job."

"That's wonderful!" Ida Mae said, giving Anne a smile of support. She admired the woman's guts—Anne had to know she'd been the talk of the town, and to take the bull by the horns like that—Arlette would be proud.

And in fact, she was. As soon as Ida Mae sat down, Arlette whispered in her ear, "Good for Anne. She tackled that head on."

"Yes, she did," Ida Mae murmured. "And I'm so glad."

After the lesson, she noticed several women come up to Anne and offer their congratulations. The announcement had been a gutsy move, but it was definitely the right thing to do.

○—

Monday evening finally arrived, and Eden perched on the edge of the sofa, looking much like a raven with her dark hair and black jacket. "Check this out," she said, pointing to a sheet of paper she'd pulled out of her bag. "That order was processed at nine o'clock in the morning. The only time an order should be put through by someone other than me is when I'm not there. I was there at nine o'clock. I knew I was, but I double checked. Look, here's another order, put through by me, fifteen seconds later. I was very much there. So someone else put this order for Tulsa into one of the networked computers in the building, even though it's my job to do it."

"So, they were trying to sneak it in without you knowing about it," Arlette said. "Do you think they suspect you?"

"Well, I wouldn't say they were trying to keep it from *me*, specifically—I'd say they were keeping it from everyone," Eden said. "And if they hadn't forgotten the zip code, I never would have even noticed the package. I don't think they suspect anything."

"So, you say it was a case of formula," Ida Mae said, taking notes.

"Yes, one case."

Ida Mae tapped her pencil on her notepad. "This is the only suspicious thing you've noticed so far, right?"

"Right."

"Well, we might as well start looking into it."

"How long has this Tulsa customer been ordering?" Ren asked. "Are they a long-standing customer, or are they new?"

"I didn't check," Eden said. "But I will tomorrow. That's a good idea."

He held up a hand in mock protest. "Do not flatter me, m'lady."

"Okay, so we have our assignments. Eden will check into the records and see how new this customer in Tulsa is. Ren is going to the Dunns' to check the camera tonight, and that's all we need to do. Until Eden uncovers something else, we're pretty much at loose ends." Ida Mae flipped her notebook closed. "Any questions?"

Everyone shook their heads.

"Okay. We'll see you at tomorrow's presidency meeting."

As the women filtered out, Ida Mae caught sight of Eden giving Ren a gentle slug on the shoulder. She couldn't help the smile that crossed her face.

Ren's car pulled into the driveway, but he didn't open the garage door. Ida Mae looked up from the book she was reading as he came into the house.

"I need your help," he said, raking his fingers through his hair. "The Dunns got a dog."

"Oh, no," Ida Mae said. She stuck a bookmark in her novel and stood up. "What happened?"

"Well, the dog was inside the house, so it didn't chase me or anything. But it barked something fierce as I went past, and Nick kept sticking his head out the back door to see what was going on."

"You don't think they know we've been out there, do you?" Ida Mae asked.

"I have no idea. I couldn't even check to see if the camera had been tampered with."

"What do you want me to do?"

"Well, that's the problem," Ren said. "I'm not really sure. You don't own a high-frequency dog whistle or anything, do you?"

"Of course not. And wouldn't that drive the dog even more nuts?"

"Well, I thought you could blow it on the other side of the house. You know, create a diversion."

"I've never thought to buy a dog whistle. Sorry."

Ren pulled his hair back into an elastic. "Maybe you could go up to the house and talk to the Dunns about something, and they'll think the dog is barking at you."

Ida Mae looked at the clock. It was only eight—she could probably justify a visit. "Okay," she said. "Let me change my clothes."

○—

"Oh, no," Ren said. "The dog's outside."

The animal was cute and looked friendly enough, but he was sniffing around the side of the house where Ren needed to be.

"I can't go up to the house and ask them to bring the dog inside," Ida Mae said. "That would just be weird."

They climbed back in the car and started to brainstorm. Ren suggested a tranquilizer inserted into a steak, but Ida Mae argued that they didn't have a tranquilizer, and no, she wouldn't risk trying to get the dog drunk. Someone would see them buying beer.

After ten minutes of useless bantering, Ren started the engine. "I think I know what to do," he said, and put the car in reverse.

○—

Eden squatted down on the ground outside the Dunns', her hand resting on top of a large cat carrier. Arlette was out for the evening and didn't know they'd catnapped her pet, and with any luck, she never would know. Besides, as Ren justified, they'd brought Eden along too, so Eden could be responsible for the animal. She thanked him profusely.

Ren put four fresh Ds into the battery-operated fan and positioned it behind the cat.

"And this is going to do what, again?" Ida Mae asked, questioning her nephew's sanity and not for the first time.

"Well, in theory, the fan will blow the scent of cat over to the dog, who will wander over here," Ren said. "If I figured it out right, the dog's chain is a fifty-footer, and he'll only be able to come as far as that stump, so we'll be safe."

"What if Nick comes out to investigate?" Ida Mae asked.

"Then we'll think of something. But this is the best I could do, short notice. So, you stand here and wait about five minutes, then push the *on* button. I'll go round the other side and start making my way toward the house. When I see the dog head the other direction, I'll get to the camera as fast as I can."

Ida Mae shook her head. This scheme was getting crazier by the second.

She waited about five minutes after Ren's shadowy figure disappeared into the night, then pushed the button. Eden held up her fingers.

"Testing the direction of the air," she whispered, and scooted the cat over a couple of inches.

Ida Mae could hear the dog's chain dragging against the ground, but there was no indication that he was coming closer. She squinted her eyes into the darkness, trying to see Ren, but couldn't make out anything.

"Hurry," she whispered, even though he couldn't hear her.

The sound of furious barking jolted her thoughts, and she looked up to see the dog charging toward them. It was a basset hound, and his ears dragged the ground with every step. He was awfully adorable— that is, he would have been if not for the long, slobber-covered teeth that lined his jaws and flashed white in the moonlight with every bark.

"Ren said the dog was on a fifty-foot chain, right?" Eden said.

"Yes . . ."

"He was wrong. Run!"

Eden grabbed the cat carrier, Ida Mae snatched up the fan, and they ran as fast as they could. Behind them, they heard a yip as the dog's chain hit its full length and jerked him back. They turned to see the dog fully twenty-five feet beyond where they had been standing.

"Now what?" Ida Mae whispered.

"We have to keep the dog entertained for a few minutes. Here boy! Here boy!" Eden snapped her fingers. The dog stood up and tried to come, but was yanked back by the chain again.

Up at the house, the front door opened. Nick stepped out onto the porch and looked around, then shook his head as he went back inside.

Ida Mae took a deep breath. Thankfully, Nick hadn't noticed anything out of place. The dog, however, didn't seem to know what to do. He looked back at the house, then at Eden, who was still holding her hand out to him. He settled by sitting down, looking at them, and whimpering.

Moments later, Ren's dark form materialized in the trees behind them, his sudden appearance giving Ida Mae a start.

"I changed the film in the camera," he said. "Let's go." He picked up the cat carrier and the fan effortlessly. Ida Mae bit back a retort. She and Eden had really struggled with those two items.

"How did it go?" he asked once they were all in the car.

"The chain was a seventy-five footer," Ida Mae told him.

"Really? I could have sworn fifty," he said, sounding unconcerned.

"Your dear old auntie was almost made into a chew toy tonight!" she continued, trying to raise any kind of guilt in him at all.

"You did great," he said instead, looking very unremorseful.

"And we could have lost Arlette's cat," she added.

"That would indeed have been a shame."

Eden reached out and slugged his shoulder. "Why are you being so smug? And what took you so long?"

Ren reached into his pocket and pulled out the film. "While I was changing the film in the camera, the black Jaguar pulled into the drive. I hadn't taken the old film out yet, and I snapped a picture of the car as it went past. If I am right, I just took a picture of the driver."

Ida Mae opened her mouth to congratulate him, but a loud yowl filled the air, and Eden swore. It wasn't one of the worst swear words, but it *was* one, nonetheless.

"Sorry," she said.

Ida Mae turned to see Eden holding onto her hand. "The cat looked uncomfortable, so I reached in there to pet him, and the beast scratched me. Ungrateful wretch."

Ida Mae fumbled in her bag and pulled out a foil package of Neosporin and some Band-Aids. "Here you go, dear."

"Are you prepared or what?" Eden took the items and got to work nursing herself as Ren pulled the car onto the road.

○—

Upon reaching the house, Eden and Ida Mae fidgeted in the living room while Ren worked his magic in the bathroom-turned-darkroom.

"It's taking forever," Eden said, falling onto the couch.

"It's only been a little while, but I agree that it does feel like forever," Ida Mae said.

Eden sat motionless for a couple of minutes, then stood to wander around the room. She stopped at the fireplace and studied the row of framed pictures that sat on the mantle.

"You've got a really nice-looking family," she said, picking up the picture of Ida Mae with her two children. "Where do they live now?"

"Keith lives in Montana, and Kim is in Detroit," Ida Mae said. "That picture was taken several years ago."

"They're both quite a long ways away." Eden replaced the picture, unaware of the discomfort Ida Mae felt. "Do you have grandchildren?"

"They each have two of their own. All boys."

"You must be very proud." She continued down the fireplace, peering at the faces in the pictures.

"I am proud . . . of them. I'm not so proud of myself." Ida Mae didn't know she was going to say the words until they were out, dangling in the air where she couldn't snatch them back. She felt her cheeks grow warm, and she took a sip of the ice water she'd served upon reaching the house.

"What do you mean?" Eden asked, turning to face Ida Mae. "Unless you don't want to tell me. I understand."

Ida Mae was tempted to pretend she hadn't said anything, but at the same time, she found the idea of sharing . . . appealing. She was used to shouldering the burdens of others. Wouldn't it be nice for just a few, small minutes, to share a burden of her own?

"I've always been a caretaker," she said, shifting a little in her chair. "It's how I was raised. When my children came along, I loved watching over them and seeing to their every little need. When they got older, I guess I was still trying to do what I'd always done." Ida Mae took a deep breath, the memory of that day coming back sharply. "They sat me down, together, and told me that they wanted to live their own lives. They were tired of me trying to do it for them. And they left."

"I'm sorry," Eden said when Ida Mae fell silent.

"I thought I was just being a good mother," Ida Mae said. "I didn't realize I was smothering them. I didn't know where the line was. I didn't even know there was a line. They say they've accepted my apologies, but they haven't been back to see me, and they haven't invited me to come out there."

Eden didn't say anything, and Ida Mae was grateful. She didn't want any platitudes or words of consolation. She wanted to be in the moment, to feel the weight of what she'd just said aloud for the first time.

When Eden did speak, Ida Mae wasn't expecting what she said.

"I would have loved to have a mother like you."

Ida Mae looked over at the girl and was surprised to see tears on her eyelashes. "My mom was really absent. Grandma practically raised me until I was twelve, and then my dad decided to take more of a hand. But if it hadn't been for Grandma, I would have been pretty much neglected."

"Taking Ren in sort of gave me a second chance, too," Ida Mae said, knowing Eden would identify. "He's helped me feel that maybe I wasn't a total failure."

"You're not a failure." Eden walked over and placed her hand on Ida Mae's shoulder. "I've watched the way you care for the people in this town. Okay, so, you have a strange and illegal way of showing it, but you really care for them."

The door to the bathroom opened, and both Eden and Ida Mae jumped. "Well?" they said simultaneously.

"Nothing," Ren said, handing Ida Mae the picture. "There wasn't enough light. All I could make out is that he has a mustache."

Ida Mae and Eden hunched together, studying the photo. "That's about all I see, too," Eden said, and Ida Mae agreed.

"There are two men at work with mustaches," Eden said. "I can't tell who this is."

"I was so close," Ren said. He flumped down on the sofa. "I really thought I had something."

"We have a lot more than we would have had without you," Ida Mae said, inwardly grimacing at her words. Yes, they would all now have prison records. That was definitely something they had with Ren's help. But at the same time, she knew they were on to something. They just had to keep looking. Hopefully, that continued looking wouldn't involve any more cats.

Chapter 20

Eden burst in through Ida Mae's kitchen door, Ren hot on her heels. "Ida Mae!"

Ida Mae looked up from the coupons she was clipping. "Yes, dear?"

"Look at this!" She pulled up a chair and plopped down, setting a piece of paper on the table. "Okay. Nick shipped out that package to Tulsa, right? Well, here's the thing. When you're through shipping a package, you're supposed to put the order sheet into a box on my desk. That sheet hasn't shown up, and it's been a couple of days."

"And no one else would have taken it out?" Ida Mae asked.

"Nope. That's my job." Eden jabbed the paper with her finger. "See what this means? Someone placed the order without my knowledge and they didn't file the order form properly. And . . ." she paused, probably for dramatic effect.

"And?" Ida Mae prompted on cue.

"The order is no longer in the computer's database."

"What?"

"Someone went in and erased it," Ren put in. "There is now no record of that package, except with the shipping company."

"Why put it in the computer at all?" Ida Mae asked.

"To print the shipping label," Eden explained. "You have to fill out a form on the computer in order to print the label. If Nick tried to mail a package without the right shipping label, it would really call attention to itself. I bet the guy in the Jaguar put the order into the computer to get the label, had Nick fill the order, and then erased all evidence of it from the computer. Nick probably destroyed the form instead of returning it to my box."

"So, Nick *is* illegally shipping something," Ida Mae said. "He's not stealing baby formula, is he?"

"I don't think so," Ren said. "That certainly wouldn't bring in the kind of cash he's had lately. I think he's shipping drugs."

"Drugs?" Ida Mae blinked. "Are you sure?"

"Think about it," Ren said, shoving his hands into

his pockets. "He's shipping something under the radar. It's bringing in cash every ten days. What else could it be? Nothing else that valuable is small enough to ship in formula canisters. Unless we're talking about jewels, but no one really steals and sells jewels anymore. That's kind of a James Bond thing."

"Does Nick know what he's doing?" Ida Mae asked.

"It's possible they didn't tell him exactly what he was shipping, but he has to know it's wrong. Nobody pays you under the table for doing something legal. Besides, remember that conversation we taped between him and Mary? She said it wasn't right. So, she knows a little something about it, too."

Ida Mae shook her head, trying to squelch down the sick feeling that was building in her stomach. This meant jail time for Nick and Mary. What would happen to the children? For a second, she wished the Secret Sisters had never gotten involved, with all their high-tech gadgets. But it was only a matter of time before the law got wind of it anyway, regardless of who brought it to light.

"What do we do?" she asked, feeling the weight of the decision.

"We still can't do anything," Ren said. "All this is conjecture. We have no proof of anything."

"Back to square one, then?"

"Not exactly," Eden said. "We know a lot more than we did. We just don't have proof of it, that's all."

"I wish someone would make a mistake so we could turn the whole thing over to the police," Ida Mae said. She pushed her chair back from the table and reached for the emergency can of soda pop she kept on the shelf just for times like this. Her stomach needed some attention, fast.

"You all right, Auntie?"

"I'm fine, Ren. I just feel a little sick, that's all." She poured the pop over some ice and began to sip. "I can't stand the thought of Nick and Mary ending up in jail and those poor children being farmed out somewhere."

"I can't promise you that won't happen," Ren said. "But I do know this. The sooner we can get to the bottom of this, the better for everyone."

○—

"I have something to report," Eden said, her cheeks pink with excitement. "James Jeffries asked me out to dinner tomorrow night."

"The man in the Jaguar?" Arlette pressed her lips together. "That can't be a good idea."

"Oh, but it is!" Eden said, patting her grandmother on the arm. "I might be able to find out what's really going on."

"How did this come about?" Ida Mae asked.

"Well, I think Nichole—you know, the girl I asked about the car? I think she must have told him I showed some interest, because last week he came down to my desk and introduced himself to me. A few times since then, he's walked by and said hello, and today, just before I left, he asked me out."

"And you said?" Arlette asked.

"I said yes, of course. I'd be crazy not to."

"Well, I think you're crazy *to* say yes," Arlette told her.

"We can follow her," Ida Mae pointed out. "Where is he taking you?"

"To Laserre," she said. "I told him I'd meet him there at five."

"Good girl," Tansy said. "Meeting him there is such a smart idea."

"Laserre?" Ida Mae blinked. "That new French restaurant in Salt Lake?"

"That's the one."

"I've heard it's terribly expensive."

"Let's live it up for once," Tansy said. "We might never have the chance to eat there again."

Ida Mae considered. Tansy did have a point. And they had to protect Eden at all costs. She felt her resolve crumbling even before it had time to become cemented.

"I'll call and see if we can get a reservation," she said. She dialed and learned they could fit in her party of three—Ren had to work and would not be joining them. It was probably just as well—it would be such a shame if the boy had to watch Eden on a date with another man.

The ladies watched Eden enter the restaurant, then counted to sixty before crossing the street and entering themselves. Ida Mae looked around when they got inside—Eden must have already been seated.

"Babbitt, party of three," she told the maitre d'.

He led them through the dining room, past tables swathed in white linen. Ida Mae felt like a chick waddling after Mama Duck as he guided them to an empty table. She finally caught sight of Eden and James, off to the right, but they were nowhere near the table designated for Ida Mae's party.

"Will this be all right?" the maitre d' asked solicitously, and Ida Mae didn't think it was.

"Do you have anything . . . over there?" she asked, nodding in Eden's direction. "The sunlight on this table . . . is too bright." She knew her excuse was pathetic, but it was the only thing she could think of.

He looked at the table, and at the window. "Too bright?"

Ida Mae realized the sun was setting and felt very uncomfortable all of a sudden, but she had to carry on bravely. "Yes. I can't be subjected to too much light."

"She gets blotchy," Tansy interjected.

"More blotchy than she is now," Arlette added.

"I'll see what I can do. Please wait here."

He moved through the tables and looked around, then was back. "I believe I found just the thing," he said. "Please, come this way."

He situated them at a table several feet away from Eden's, but she was now close enough that she could signal if need be. Ida Mae breathed a sigh of relief and picked up her menu.

"I'm not blotchy," she said to Arlette, skimming through the entrée selections.

"You do get a little spotty under the eyes when you haven't had enough sleep," Arlette replied.

"Then you should pity me, not share the information with the world at large."

"It got us this table, didn't it?"

They looked at their choices for a moment, then Tansy said, "Don't look now, but they're both standing up."

Arlette started to put her menu down, but Tansy hissed, "I said don't look!"

All three women held their menus high, but peeked around the edges. Sure enough, James and Eden were walking away, led by the maitre d'.

"They aren't leaving, are they?" Tansy asked.

"I think they're sitting at that other table," Arlette replied.

They watched as Eden took her seat at a table near the fireplace.

"Well, now what are we going to do? She's clear over there, and we're clear over here," Tansy said.

Ida Mae raised her hand. The maitre d' saw and scurried over.

"What can I do for you?"

"I . . . I'm getting a little chilled. Would it be possible for us to move closer to the fire?"

"She does get very cold," Tansy said.

"She's downright icy sometimes," Arlette added.

He tilted his head to the side. "The fire might give off light, madam. Is that all right?"

"It's sunlight I'm allergic to. Firelight is perfectly fine."

"I'll see what I can do."

Once again, he scurried off to check for tables. Once again, he came back. "You are in luck. I do have one table."

"Take your menus," Ida Mae whispered, and the ladies tucked them under their arms as they rose. They had to pass Eden's table to get to their own, and they held their menus high, pretending to study them as they passed.

"Here you are," the maitre d' said, helping the ladies be seated. "Is there anything else I can do for you?"

"This is perfect," Ida Mae said.

"Very well. I'll send your waiter over shortly."

The three nibbled bread and peeked at Eden while they waited for their entrees. Eden seemed to be having a good time. Her light laughter filled the room from time to time, and James seemed very attentive. If Ida Mae hadn't known he was full of evil, she would have said he was downright charming.

Right after Ida Mae's roast beef arrived, James got a call on his cell phone. He excused himself to go answer it, and stepped out into the hall.

"This might be important," Tansy whispered. "One of us should go listen in."

"I'll go," Ida Mae said. "My dinner needs a minute to cool anyway."

She rose and walked toward the hallway, thinking she could pretend to be on her way to the ladies' room. But when she got there, she saw that she was in a corridor that led directly to the kitchen, with no ladies' room in sight, no pay phone—no logical reason for her to be there. There was, however, a large potted plant in the corner. She dove behind it just as James, who was facing away from her, turned on his heel and started pacing back the other way.

"I don't know why you think that," he said into the phone. "I've done everything you asked me to do."

Ida Mae crouched, trying to ignore the fact that the plant was some variety of fern, and she was allergic to most types of fern.

"I think it's only my right," James continued. "I've done all the legwork, haven't I?"

Ida Mae tried to ignore the fact that the plant was set in some sort of peat moss, and she was allergic to most types of peat moss.

"We'll have to talk about this on Monday," James continued. "I'm at dinner right now, and I need to get back to my table. Yes, I'm with a woman. It's none of your business who." He listened for another minute, and then snapped, "I said we'd talk on Monday." He shut his phone, snapping it like a castanet, then strode back into the dining room.

Ida Mae began to straighten from her hiding spot, then startled at a voice behind her. The maitre d' had come up and was inquiring what she might need.

"I was just looking for the ladies' room," she said.

"If you go out through the dining room, you'll find it to the left," he said. "I'm afraid there's nothing back here but the kitchen and an emergency exit."

"Thank you," she said, and made her way back out to the dining room, where she took her seat and checked her food. It was now just right.

"What happened?" Tansy asked, just as Ida Mae let loose a long-restrained "A-a-a-choo!"

"May I offer you a tissue and an antihistamine?" the maitre d' asked, appearing at her elbow. She didn't appreciate the touch of sarcasm in his voice.

○━

"Why did you change tables?" Arlette asked later that night as they gathered at Ida Mae's to compare notes.

"James said he wanted to sit somewhere a little more intimate," Eden explained. "We couldn't really hear each other talk where we were at first."

"I'm just glad we were able to change tables too," Ida Mae said. "I would have felt terrible if you hadn't been in our line of sight."

"I was giving thought to rigging semaphore flags with two napkins and a couple of long breadsticks, but you solved that by moving, too," Eden told her.

"So, what did you find out?" Tansy asked. Ren hadn't said anything yet. If Ida Mae had to describe the look on his face, she would say he glowered.

"Nothing much, really. James has worked for the company for about two years, moved here from New York, likes the area, and he enjoys salmon."

"That's it?" Tansy sounded disappointed.

"Well, his Jaguar's about a year old. He had it shipped out from New York."

"Why New York?" Tansy asked. "Couldn't he find one a little closer to home?"

"I guess he has a friend who owns a dealership and gave him a special price," Eden said. "He's very proud of that car. He even gave it a name—Elvira."

"Elvira?" Ida Mae asked. "What kind of name is that?"

"I named my first car," Eden said. "It had problems with the shocks and every time it went over a bump, it bounced, so I named it Tigger."

Everyone nodded their approval of her wise choice.

"What about you, Ida Mae?" Arlette asked. "What did you find out when you went to eavesdrop?"

Ida Mae leaned forward a little, eager to share as she recounted what she'd overheard.

"That sounds very promising," Arlette said. "Definitely suspicious."

"I thought so too," Ida Mae said. She pulled out her pad and made notes on everything they'd said. "Now, Eden, are you going to keep dating James?"

"I don't know. He said he had a good time and he'd like to call me, so I guess we'll see."

"Whatever happens, be sure to tell us whenever you go somewhere with him," Ida Mae said. "We'll want to be on hand at all times."

"I will," Eden replied.

And Ren continued to glower.

Chapter 21

With all the excitement of the Friday night date, plus the long list of Saturday chores behind her, Ida Mae thought she'd go right to sleep Saturday night. But she was too tired to relax. She had gone to bed early, feeling tired down to the marrow of her bones, but her brain wouldn't settle down and let her drift off. She tightened the sash of her robe and went downstairs, thinking a mug of chamomile tea might do the trick. While waiting for the water to heat, she flipped on the small TV she kept on the counter. No, she didn't want a talk show. No, not an old sitcom. No, she wasn't in the mood to buy a bracelet that was perfect to wear while grocery shopping. She settled on the news, and watched while her tea bag bobbed in the water.

"And that's it for sports," said the plastic-haired anchorman. "In local news, we have just learned that a black Jaguar drove off the road and into the river near Parley's Pass just outside of Omni. The driver was killed. It's too soon for more information, but join us at six for our morning broadcast, and we'll see what we can find out."

Ida Mae gasped. There couldn't be another black Jaguar in the area, not out here in Omni.

When Ren came in from his late work shift, he agreed with her. "It has to be the same car," he said. "Parley's Pass is just ten miles from here. It can't be a coincidence."

"So, what do we do?" Ida Mae asked, feeling for the first time in her life like she wasn't in control.

"I guess we wait and see what Eden finds out at the warehouse on Monday," he said, raking his hand through his hair. As he did, Ida Mae noticed something—or rather, *didn't* notice something.

"Ren, where's your earring?"

He smiled and ducked his head. "Eden said she wondered what I'd look like without it, so I took it out."

"And did she like what she saw?" Ida Mae asked, suppressing a smile.

"I guess. She kissed my cheek."

His face was now the color of a raspberry.

Ida Mae figured she'd better not add to his embarrassment, but she couldn't help but say, "I like you better without, too." But she didn't kiss his cheek—she might smudge Eden's.

Ren glanced at the clock. "I'm going to go out to the Dunns' to check on the camera," he said. "I haven't been out there since the other night with the cat."

"It's ten-thirty," Ida Mae told him. "And we've got church in the morning."

"I won't be long," he said. "I just want to see what's been going on."

"What about the dog?"

He held up a silver cylinder. The boy had gotten his hands on a dog whistle. She didn't even want to think about it.

Ida Mae dumped her tea down the sink after he left—there was no point in trying to sleep now. She wouldn't be able to relax until she heard what Ren had discovered. She pulled out her Relief Society lesson manual from her church bag and settled in to study, trying to keep her mind on the topic at hand but found herself startling every time she heard a sound.

A half hour later, Ren came in the house.

"What did you find?" she asked, setting the book off to the side.

"Several pictures were taken," he said. "I'll need to develop them in order to find out what's going on."

"But it's almost midnight. It's bad enough that we're skulking around like thieves—we probably shouldn't develop this film until Monday morning."

Ren scuffed the carpet with his toe, looking for all the world like a little boy who's been told he can't go out on the playground.

"On the other hand," she said, "if we discover something that could help the police . . ."

Ren brightened instantly and headed for the darkroom. "I'll be out as fast as I can."

Now I've done it, Ida Mae thought as she settled back in her chair. *First I'm a criminal, now I'm aiding and abetting Sabbath breaking. Don't ask me how I'm going to explain any of this to Bishop Sylvester. And him with his new babies and all.*

The triplets had been born and were doing well, with very few complications. They would be coming home from the hospital in a few days, and she had spent an hour that day coordinating meals.

She thought she was too wired to rest, but must have dozed off. The next thing she knew, Ren was coming out of the bathroom, holding some pictures in his hands. The clock struck midnight, and she almost congratulated him on getting the work done before the Sabbath hit, but a look at his face told her he'd discovered something important.

"This is very interesting," Ren said. "I could tell the camera had taken several shots, but I thought it must have been birds or something setting off the shutter. But look." He spread the prints out on the coffee table.

Ida Mae rose from her chair and studied the prints. The first was of Nick, facing right. The next was of Nick, facing left. Then right, then left.

"I don't understand," she said.

"Look at the timestamps."

The pictures were all from that night. The first was taken at 20:55:05, the second at 20:55:10, and the third at 20:55:15. "They're all five seconds apart," she said.

"Right."

"So, he's . . . pacing?"

"Exactly." Ren pointed to Nick's face. "He's looking around, and see in this one—he looks upset. He's pacing."

"So he's outside, and he's upset and pacing." Ida Mae suddenly realized the implications. "He was waiting for the Jaguar, which didn't come because it drove into the river instead."

"Score one for the blue-haired lady," Ren said, patting her shoulder. "I think we have proof positive

225

that our man in the river is the man who's been meeting Nick out back of their house."

"Proof enough for us," Ida Mae said. She picked up the picture that showed Nick's face most clearly and sat down, studying it. "The police will never believe us."

"Then we'll keep digging until we *make* them believe us," Ren said. "But we've got an even bigger problem now."

"What's that?"

Ren's usually cheerful face was solemn. "We don't know if the accident was really an accident, or if the man in the Jaguar was murdered. And if he was murdered, there's someone else behind this, someone even more powerful. And if that someone catches wind of what Eden's doing there, she could be in danger too."

○—

"I'm not quitting."

"Yes, you are."

"No, I'm not." Eden reached out and grabbed a cookie off the plate in the center of the table, either unaware or not caring that every set of eyes in the room was firmly fixed on her. Ida Mae had promised to keep her mouth shut and let Ren do all the talking, but it was proving very difficult.

"Eden, there's been a murder," Ren said. "We're talking about lives here."

"Maybe James had a little too much Kool-Aid and misjudged the turn," Eden replied.

"But what are the odds of that happening? We've got a car that's been making deliveries of pretty substantial amounts of money. We're investigating shady dealings at the company where this car spends a lot of time in the parking lot, and now that car's been fished out of the river, and the driver is dead. What are the odds, Eden?"

"But who's the murderer? We don't even have reason to be suspicious of anyone else."

"Which brings me back to the point of this whole discussion," Ren said. He caught Eden's hand as she reached for another cookie, and held her fingers in his own. "Eden, we don't know who's behind all this, and we're worried about you. Please, quit your job."

"But that would look suspicious," she said. "Listen, I know you're worried. But how would it look if I quit right after James goes into the river? Sure, it might look like I was just worried or maybe grief-stricken, I don't know, but if the person behind all this were to get suspicious, I'd lead him right back to you. Besides, we haven't done what we set out to do. We still don't know what Nick is doing. Don't we want to get to the bottom of this?"

"Shouldn't we at least consider the idea that it *wasn't* a murder?" Ida Mae said. "Cars do go off roads, you know."

"We weren't born yesterday," Arlette told her.

"I know," Ida Mae said. "I'm just trying to think like the sheriff, what objections he'd pose."

"Ida Mae, you know we're supposed to let virtue garnish our thoughts unceasingly," Arlette told her, shaking a knitting needle. "You get your thoughts away from the sheriff's brain right this instant."

"There's one more thing," Ida Mae said. "James was Nick's contact. Is Nick next on the list?"

"That clinches it for me," Eden said, pulling her hand from Ren's grasp. "I can't quit yet. Nick's life might be in danger. You started this to keep his children from going hungry—let's finish it to keep them from going fatherless."

"I told you she was going to be a writer," Arlette said, pride evident on her face.

Ida Mae had to admit, the girl could turn a phrase. She nearly expected Arlette to pull out a flag and start singing the national anthem, but she didn't.

"Very well," Ida Mae said at last. "But we'll have to get much more careful. Eden will need backup at all times. She could be going to work every day with a murderer."

"No *could be* about it, Aunt Ida Mae," Ren said. "We have to assume that's exactly what's happening. Remember the phone call you overheard James take? He does answer to someone else."

Everyone in the room nodded.

"I'm going to request a leave of absence from work," he continued. "I'm the only one here in a position to stake out the warehouse. I can sit in my car across the street. There's a parking lot there that would be perfect."

Ida Mae opened her mouth to argue, but closed it again. The boy had a point. She had her responsibilities, as did the other ladies, and she couldn't be hustling off to Salt Lake at the crack of dawn every day. She wanted Ren to keep his job, but this was so much more important. If they were dealing with murderers, something had to be done, and they still didn't have enough evidence to take to the police. She still smarted from how Ricky Shelton teased her over the Wendy's wrapper—she could just imagine the ridicule she'd get if she showed him the pictures of Nick pacing.

"My boss is really cool," Ren said, and Ida Mae realized she hadn't been listening. "If I tell him I need some personal time, I think he'll understand."

"That's good of you, Ren," Tansy said, patting his shoulder. "I pledge to supply you with lots of food to eat in the car."

"And I'll throw in the brownies," Arlette said.

The moment was broken when Hannah slipped into the room. "Sorry I'm late," she said. "We had a check-up for Joey, and I just got back."

"How is he?" Ida Mae asked.

"Much, much better," she replied. "What did I miss?"

Tansy quickly filled her in, and Hannah nodded. "We've definitely got to keep investigating," she said. "Something really bad could happen if we don't."

"And at the first real evidence we get, we're heading straight for the police, right?" Arlette said.

"Yes. And you can be the one to call them," Ida Mae promised. No way was she putting herself through *that* again.

"Oh, no!" Tansy cried out a moment later. "I bet the money got all wet!"

"The money?" Ida Mae asked.

"The money James was bringing to Nick. It went into the river with the car, didn't it? I bet it's all wet and soggy and ruined. What will they do at the bank?"

"I'm sure they have a way to take care of it," Ida Mae reassured her. She nearly made a comment about money laundering, but kept it to herself.

"You don't think they'll have to iron it, do you?" Tansy asked. "I bet they'd use the wrong setting."

○—

"Aunt Ida Mae, help me test this," Ren said, walking into the kitchen with a small object in his hand. He held it up, and Ida Mae gasped. It was a beautiful brooch in the shape of a cat, with sparkling crystals embedded in it.

"Do you think Eden will like it?" he asked.

Ida Mae's heart melted. Her dear boy was preparing to give a gift to his lady friend—it was so sweet.

"I think she'll love it, dear," she said, patting his cheek.

"Good, because she's going to wear it every day."

Ida Mae blinked. "What?" Surely he didn't think he could dictate how often Eden wore it. It was a gift, after all.

"It's a communicator. I call it a commlink. You push these buttons and it activates an alarm on the watch I'm wearing. I'm very proud of myself."

"As well you should be." Ida Mae tried to squelch her disappointment. Was it wrong for her to want Ren to find happiness in his life? And Eden was such a nice girl, although she wasn't terribly pleased with the idea of having Arlette as an in-law.

"I'm going to stand outside. You push the buttons, okay? First, push the cat's left eye, then his right, then his nose, then his stomach. Got that?"

"Left, right, nose, stomach. Why so many buttons?"

"Well, if the alarm triggered with just one button, she could set it off accidentally. If it was two buttons, she could still set it off, if she pushed them within a few minutes of each other. But four, the odds are significantly lower. Now, what was that order again?"

"Left, right, nose, stomach."

"Very good. Give me about two minutes."

Ren slipped out the door and Ida Mae counted out two minutes. Then she pushed the tiny buttons on the cat, which were placed behind the crystals. It was ingenious.

"It worked!" Ren dashed in, leaping around in a victory dance.

"Arlette and Eden are coming over tonight for dinner," she said, watching Ren carefully to gauge his reaction.

"Good. I can give her the pin then," he replied,

not having the decency to blush or stammer or even look embarrassed. Ida Mae turned away in frustration. There had to be a way to make him admit his feelings. That is, if he had feelings, which she was sure he did. How could he not?

○—

"Now, you only activate this if it's the most dire emergency," Ren said. "If my watch alarm goes off, I'm going to assume you're either dead or dying, and I'll act accordingly."

"By making funeral potatoes?" Eden asked with a smirk.

"Yeah. Just joke about life and death like that, young lady. Now, what's the sequence again?"

"Left eye, then the right eye, then the stomach—"

"No, the nose," Ren said.

"Left eye, right eye, nose, and stomach," Eden recited. He made her say it five more times before he was satisfied.

"What if she gets the order wrong?" Ida Mae asked.

"She won't," Arlette interjected. "She's as smart as a whip."

"Theoretically, what if she pushes the wrong sequence?"

"Nothing. It just won't set off the alarm."

"Left eye, right eye, nose and stomach." Eden pinned the cat on her sweater just below her left collarbone. "This is an awfully pretty pin, Ren. I'm glad you didn't use something dreadful, like a skull."

"Well, I know how much you like cats," he said, looking at Ida Mae over Arlette's head. They had all agreed not to tell Arlette about their adventure with her cat, but it was very hard to maintain a straight face in that lady's presence. Eden's lips twitched dangerously, and Ida Mae leaped to the rescue.

"Does anyone want dessert?"

"I do!" Eden said, jumping out of her chair a little too eagerly. "I'll come help serve."

Ida Mae set Eden to cutting the brownies while she pulled out the ice cream. "We're very worried about you, Eden. Are you sure you want to keep working at the warehouse?"

"You couldn't pay me to stop," Eden said. "I'm really having so much fun, sleuthing on the sly. And I haven't found anything yet, so it's not like they have to kill me to keep me from blabbing."

"Seriously, dear, I'm concerned."

Eden placed her hand on Ida Mae's shoulder. "Thank you for worrying about me. It means a lot. I admit, James's death did shake me up a little, but I promise you, I'm going to be fine."

Ida Mae studied the girl's serious brown eyes, then nodded. "If you're sure."

"I am."

Ida Mae turned back to the ice cream and scooped a generous portion into each bowl. To her, the evidence was as clear as the nose on Bob Hope's face. But until they came up with a little more, the police wouldn't believe them. She hoped they would be able to find the answers soon before things got entirely out of control.

Chapter 22

Ren left early to take up his post across the street from the warehouse. Ida Mae had packed him a substantial lunch, Arlette threw in some brownies, and Tansy stayed up half the night making a potato salad. They were all pitching in the best way they knew how, wishing they could do more.

Ren and Ida Mae discussed things before he left, and while Ida Mae didn't like it, she had to agree that things were going to have to be brought to a head. With James Jeffries coming up dead, their investigation would have to take a more serious turn. Eden would be doing even more digging, and the stakes were higher than ever.

Eden got home around the same time that night and came straight to Ida Mae's, with Ren just a couple minutes behind her. Arlette and Tansy were already there, and had been for half an hour, anxiously awaiting news. Arlette had even dropped a stitch and had to go back to pick it up, she was so rattled.

"They called us together for a company meeting this morning," Eden told them after she took a long sip of water. "They announced that James Jeffries was killed in a car accident on Saturday night, and today they brought in his replacement. I thought that was really weird. James is killed on Saturday, here it is Monday, and they've already replaced him?"

"Sounds like they knew he was going to die," Ren said, running his hand through his hair. Ida Mae almost gasped when he did it—at some point between the time he left the house that morning and returned to it ten minutes ago, he'd gotten his hair cut. She was glad, but she was shocked. What had gotten into the boy all of a sudden?

"That's what I thought. Maybe they had to get rid of him to make room for this new guy," Eden said. "His name is Ryan Yates, and he seems decent enough, but I don't know if he's just taking over the VP job or if he's going to start making Nick's deliveries, too. I mean, just how many of James's duties will he be taking over? Or was James killed to keep him from making more deliveries?"

Ida Mae jotted everything down on her list. "Were you able to find out anything else?" she asked.

Eden shook her head. "Tomorrow *is* another day, you know."

"Did you have enough food?" Tansy asked Ren.

"I had more than enough, thank you," he said, patting his stomach. "I'm going to have to cut down tomorrow—if Eden had needed me, I don't think I would have been able to run, I was so full."

Tansy beamed. "I'll make you a nice turkey sandwich on dry wheat tomorrow, then," she said.

"You don't have to go *that* far," he protested.

The meeting came to an end, and the ladies went out to their cars. Ren excused himself to go to bed, but Ida Mae held up her hand.

"Just when did you have your hair cut, young man? You were supposed to be keeping an eye on Eden, not gallivanting around looking for beauty parlors."

"I kept my eye on her the whole time. In fact, she went with me on her lunch hour."

"And just what prompted this change of heart?"

"She said she wondered what I'd look like with short hair."

"And did she give you another kiss on the cheek?"

Ren's face broke in half with his smile. "Or something like that."

Ren went to his room and Ida Mae to hers, but not to sleep. Honestly, she couldn't decide if she was an insomniac or a narcoleptic. When she was tired, it was all she could do to stay awake long enough to find her bed, but there were nights when she couldn't seem to sleep at all. She refused to think that age might have anything to do with it. It simply wasn't a factor.

O—

The next day, Ida Mae felt much better. With her new visiting teaching assignments made and her phone calls complete, she tried to concentrate on making dinner. She thought she'd assemble some chicken enchiladas, but found herself staring into the fridge, forgetting what she'd gone in for. Something didn't feel right, and she recognized that sensation. Closing the fridge, she turned to the phone, hitting "1" on her speed dial.

"Arlette, it's Ida Mae," she said, bending to put on her shoes while she talked. "I've got a feeling something's not right at the warehouse, and I want to go check on Ren."

"I'm glad you called," Arlette replied. "I've been feeling the same way, and was trying to talk myself out of it."

"We can't both be having a senior moment at the exact same time," Ida Mae said. "I think we'd best get to Salt Lake City."

Arlette arranged to pick Tansy up and then come for Ida Mae in a couple of minutes. While she waited, Ida Mae looked around for something she could use as a weapon, should the need arise. The first thing she saw was her heavy cast iron skillet, which hung over her stove. She grabbed it and swung it back and forth experimentally. Okay, she was no Boris Becker, but it would have to do.

As soon as Arlette's van pulled into the drive, Ida Mae tugged her front door closed and stepped off the porch. Tansy was already in the backseat, so Ida Mae rode shotgun. She couldn't blame Arlette for backing into the street a little too quickly, or for speeding down a residential road, or even for doing a rolling stop at the four-way. Nor could she blame herself for the way her knuckles turned white when she gripped the door handle in an effort to keep her balance.

Ida Mae's premonitions of danger increased as they hit the freeway, and she knew they needed to get to Ren's side as soon as they possibly could.

Arlette's cell phone rang just as they hit the edge of Salt Lake City, and Ida Mae picked it up for her.

"Auntie? It's Ren," he said, sounding breathless. "Eden just activated her commlink."

"We're almost there," Ida Mae said.

Ninety seconds later—she knew, because she'd been counting—they pulled up in the parking lot across from the warehouse, where Ren's car was waiting. Ren himself stood on the pavement, staring at the building.

"Everyone's gone home for the night, except for Eden," he said, pointing at the employee parking lot, where only Eden's red VW waited.

Ida Mae punched numbers into Arlette's cell phone and waited impatiently for the dispatcher at the Omni Sheriff's Office to pick up.

"Hello, Lurlene? I need to talk to Ricky," she said.

"Ida Mae, is that you? Ricky's not in. He's been at a conference all day."

"Well, I really need to talk to him."

"Seein' as how it's you, you can call him on his cell. You sure it's business related?"

"Very sure."

"Okay, here's the number." Ida Mae heard a sound that could only be Lurlene popping her gum. "Here you go."

"Thanks, Lurlene." Ida Mae hung up and dialed the new number.

"Ida Mae?" Ricky's voice sounded distorted. "What in the blue blazes . . ."

"Eden activated her commlink," she told him, and waited fully three seconds for a response.

"Who? Did what?"

"Oh, never mind. But we need you!"

"Just where are you?"

She gave him the address.

"Ida Mae, that's not even in my jurisdiction! You're in Salt Lake County now. Call the Salt Lake Police."

"But I know you," she reasoned. "I don't know them."

His sigh of exasperation came through loud and clear. "I don't know what you think is going on there, but if you really need some help, you'd better call the Salt Lake Police, all right? Listen, I've hit some traffic. I'm on the road. I'll talk to you later."

Ida Mae shut the phone. "He's not coming."

"And he'd probably need more proof anyway," Tansy added.

"I guess it's up to us," Arlette said, looking resolute. "Let's go." They walked across the street, looking both ways for cars and mobsters.

"What kind of security system does this place have?" Ida Mae asked.

"Eden said they just use locks on the doors, and there's a guard dog at night," Ren said. "But I don't think the door nearest the parking lot is locked."

They sidled up to the building. Ren grabbed the handle and tugged to find that the door was open. Ida Mae flinched, expecting a loud squeal, but the hinges were silent as they trooped inside. There were no lights on in the dim building, so she pulled out the small flashlight attached to her keychain.

They were surrounded by shelves and cabinets. "Now what do we do?" Tansy asked.

"I saw movement in the northwest upper corner window just before the commlink went off," Ren said. They edged their way around the cabinets to the corner in question, and saw a flight of stairs.

Just as they were getting ready to go up, a shadowy figure dashed down the stairs pell-mell. Ren made a flying leap and landed on top of the fleeing person, who said, "Ooooph!"

Ida Mae shone her light in the newcomer's face. "It's Nick!"

Nick sat up and looked around. "I've got to call the police," he said. "They've got the new secretary in their office, and they're threatening her."

"And we've finally got a witness," Arlette said, pulling out her cell phone and punching some numbers. She spoke urgently while Ida Mae resumed her questioning.

"What's going on up there? Is Eden hurt?"

"No, but they're getting pretty mean. I heard them through the door." Nick's brow furrowed as if he was seeing them all for the first time. "Sister Babbitt, why is the Relief Society here?"

"I'll explain it later," she said. "Right now we've got to help Eden."

Ren's face looked hard in the faint light, and Ida Mae knew that expression. He was trying to stay calm, but she knew he would go charging off like a bull if provoked.

As they started up the stairs, they heard a gunshot.

Ren was provoked.

Dashing up the rest of the flight with Nick right behind him, Ren reached the top before anyone else. Ida Mae was quite amazed at the sudden burst of energy she felt as she followed along. At the top of the stairs, they came to a long hallway and saw an office door at the end. She raised her skillet high. Arlette's knitting needles were at the ready. They all burst through the door at nearly the same time, the adrenaline coursing through their veins.

Ren tackled the man just inside the door. Ida Mae fleetingly wondered if Ren was living out all his old childhood linebacker fantasies in one evening before she brought her skillet down over the head of the man standing opposite. Nick grabbed the third man in the room, and it was all over so quickly, no one had time to react. The first man's gun skittered across the floor to stop at Arlette's feet, and she picked it up, waving it around wildly. "Where's my granddaughter?" she demanded.

"I'm okay, Grandma," Eden said, speaking from the corner. "I'm not hurt."

"Then what was that shot?" Arlette asked.

"I think a car backfired outside," Eden replied. "But I'm glad you're here. These guys were about to take me on a ride."

Ida Mae took some yarn out of Arlette's bag, and they got to work trussing up the suited serpents. One of the men tried to sit up, but he took one look at the nervous grip Arlette had on the gun and decided against it.

Another man kept protesting. "You've got this all wrong," he said, trying to smile.

Ida Mae pulled out one of Arlette's newly finished creations and shoved it in his mouth. "Put a sock in it," she said.

Just then, blue and red flashing lights reflected on the wall as the Salt Lake City police pulled into the warehouse parking lot. Ida Mae heard footsteps as the officers dashed through the building and, moments later, burst into the room. She could only imagine what they must think when they saw what awaited them—three thugs, held captive by a crazed woman with a gun in one hand and a knitting needle in the other.

"Hello, officers," she said blandly, lowering her skillet at last. That thing had been getting heavy.

Ricky Shelton stepped into the room as the first men on the scene entered. "Ida Mae, what on earth . . .?"

"I tried to tell you," she said, lifting her shoulders. "But you weren't listening."

He looked around, bewilderment all over his face. He opened and closed his mouth a few times, but nothing came out.

"You look like a fish," she told him, then turned to the officers. "Yes, please do handcuff them," she said. "I trust Arlette's taste in worsted goods, but the baby yarn is a bit delicate."

The ladies moved into the hall to make room as the three suspects, plus Nick, were led out in cuffs. "We're going to need you all to come down to the station too," one officer said, and Ricky nodded.

"I'll bring them down," he said.

"I've always wanted to ride in a paddy wagon," Ida Mae told him, but he shook his head.

"We'll go in my car."

Ida Mae sighed. "That's so disappointing."

Chapter 23

Police Captain Wright hadn't said a word in twenty minutes as Ida Mae, Tansy, and Arlette filled him in on all the details of their investigation. Eden and Ren chimed in from time to time, and they laid out everything they knew. Ida Mae had the foresight to bring her notebook, and she handed it to the captain, proud of her work and her meticulous handwriting.

"I honestly don't know what to say," the captain said at long last, glancing over at Ricky, who had made himself very small in the corner. "You became suspicious because of a Wendy's wrapper?"

"Yes. That was really our first big tip-off," Ida Mae told him.

He shook his head and ran his hand across his face. "I've got some calls to make and some more questions to ask," he said. "I'm going to have you all wait in one of these other rooms."

"I hate to be a bother," Ida Mae said, "but we all missed dinner. Could we possibly step out for something to eat?"

"I'd rather keep you on the premises," the captain said. "I'll have someone go grab you a bite."

"Thank you."

Just then a tap sounded on the door.

"Come in," the captain called out, and a disheveled man stepped into the room.

"Ida Mae, I'm confused," Bishop Sylvester said.

○—

The ladies, Ren, and the bishop were shown into a conference room with padded chairs and a long table. Soon afterward, an officer bearing huge bags of fast food came in the room. "I hope you like what I got," he said. "The captain said you guys mentioned Wendy's."

"I'm sure we'll be fine," Ida Mae told him. "Thank you."

Tansy made herself the official unwrapper and arranged everything on the table according to food groups. Once they had all gathered up at least one of everything, Ida Mae turned to Eden.

"Now, just what exactly happened tonight?"

Eden held up one finger while she finished chewing her mouthful of fries. Chasing them with a swig of pop, she said, "It was pretty scary, I have to admit that."

"Well, don't leave us in suspense!" Arlette pushed her own sandwich away. She had always been too thin—Ida Mae would have liked to see another twenty pounds on her, at least. "Tell us what happened!"

"I decided I had to know the truth about James's death," Eden began. "For so long, he was just the man in the Jaguar, but after having dinner with him and getting to know him a little bit as a person, I felt responsible for solving his murder."

Tansy nodded. "That's perfectly natural."

The bishop leaned forward. "Murder?"

"We'll explain everything," Ida Mae consoled him. "Right now, we're not sure what's going on ourselves."

He leaned back, clutching his sandwich to his chest. Poor thing looked like his blood pressure was skyrocketing at that very moment. Ida Mae wondered how much sodium was in that sandwich. "Go on," she said.

"Well, I was going to see if I could sneak into his office and maybe go through his desk or something. I waited until everyone left, and then I went upstairs. I thought I was alone in the building, but then I heard voices. Before I could turn around, suddenly Mr. Phillips, the owner of the company, was in my face."

Eden took another sip of her drink. "He invited me to come in his office. I didn't know how much he knew, and I had to act natural, so I went. He had two other men in there, all big and burly—well, you saw them. He invited me to sit and then he started asking me some questions, like where I went to school and what I liked to do. Then he pulled out a picture of me having dinner with James on Friday night, taken at the restaurant, and asked me how well I knew James."

Ida Mae pulled in a sharp breath and pressed her hands together. Ren reached for another sandwich. They were both dealing with the stress in the best way they knew how.

"I explained that I had only really met James, and we'd just been on the one date. Then I pretended the clasp on my pin was broken and fiddled with it long enough to activate the commlink."

"What did he say then?" Tansy leaned forward, a dot of mustard on her chin.

"He pulled out a gun."

The bishop jumped, his sandwich taking another squishing.

"He told me they couldn't take any chances, and I'd have to come with them. He then told me I was more than welcome to share any information I had before we left."

"But there weren't any other cars in the parking lot," Tansy pointed out. "How were they planning to carry you off?"

"Mr. Phillips keeps his car in a private garage on the side of the building," Eden said. "That threw me, too, when I thought I was the only one inside. I forgot to check for his car."

"And what about Nick?" Ida Mae asked. "Where was his car?"

"He sometimes takes the bus," Eden answered sheepishly. "I didn't think of that, either."

"It's okay, dear," Ida Mae said, giving her a squeeze on the knee. "You were under a lot of stress. We understand."

"So what happened then?" Arlette prodded.

"Well, that's when you burst in," Eden said. "He was being all gruff and tough-guy like, and I was claiming my innocence, and the next thing I knew, Ren and Nick burst in, and then you guys, and it was all over."

Arlette reached out and patted her granddaughter's hand. "I'm so glad you're all right."

"Me too, Grandma."

They finished their meal in silence. The bishop recovered enough to peel his sandwich off his tie and make some effort at eating it. Ren didn't say much of anything but went through three sandwiches and two diet sodas. Ida Mae was glad to see Arlette finish hers as well. They all felt better after the rest and some nourishment, but she wouldn't feel completely at ease until they'd spoken with the police captain and figured out all the loose ends.

Chapter 24

And that's what happened," Captain Wright said three hours later.

His phone calls made, the interrogation begun, and a sandwich in his stomach, the captain looked a lot happier, Ida Mae thought. Poor Bishop Sylvester looked very much the worse for wear. She wondered if his medicine was somewhere on his person, and if they'd be able to find it if he suddenly took a fit.

"Your Relief Society presidency brought down a drug ring that's been operating in Tulsa for some time," the captain went on. "The Tulsa police have been working this case diligently but couldn't trace where the drugs were coming from. Turns out, they were being supplied from right here in Salt Lake City."

"I knew it was drugs," Ida Mae said.

"How did you know?" the captain asked her.

"Well, it was either that or diamonds, and James Bond isn't real," she explained.

Captain Wright raised an eyebrow, but didn't say anything in response. Instead, he said, "The Tulsa police have offered a substantial reward, which will be sent on to you. They are also planning to give you the key to the city in a special ceremony."

"They got that all organized so quickly?" Ida Mae asked. "I'm impressed."

"It's still being discussed," he clarified. "They'll be in touch."

"So, how did you get here so fast?" Ida Mae asked Ricky, who swallowed the remains of his third drink before replying.

"I'd been in Salt Lake all day and had just left for home when you called," he said. "I decided I'd better turn around, and when I heard the call come over the scanner, I wasn't too far away."

"Well, I'm glad you finally listened," she told him, and he went beet red.

○━

The entire membership of Secret Sisters sat on padded chairs in the stake president's office. President

Adams looked grim, but then a twinkle lit his eyes.

"This has been a most unusual case," he said, looking at the papers on the table in front of him. "I can't say as I've ever seen a group of people break so many laws, and yet do so much good at the same time. I've had to call Church headquarters to get advice on this one—there's just no precedent."

"We know we caused a lot of trouble," Ida Mae told him. "We're sorry."

"And you should be," President Adams said. "I can't believe all the sneaking and spying you did. Captain Wright told me he wasn't sure if he should hire you or have you arrested."

"We can't possibly accept the job," Arlette informed him. "It just wouldn't work out."

"I'm pretty sure he understands," President Adams said, the corners of his mouth twitching. "But sisters, we really do need to talk. I hate to do this, but I'm going to have to release you all from your callings."

"But why?" Tansy asked, her eyes filling with tears.

"You ladies have been the best Relief Society presidency the 2nd Ward has ever had, but you broke the law," President Adams said. "I can't allow you to hold positions until your debt to society has been paid."

"I understand," Ida Mae said stoically. "When do our jail terms begin?" She could probably bring enough books with her to last a few months, and she could have more brought in, and—

"You're not going to jail," President Adams said, interrupting her. "I've spent hours on the phone with the police captains in both Salt Lake City and Tulsa. I've also been in touch with Brother Mangrum in the stake—he's a lawyer, you know. He's agreed to represent you, and he's going to ask for a lighter sentence, given that you did help solve a major crime. If his plea bargain is accepted, you ladies—Eden and Hannah included—will give a thousand hours each of community service, and you'll check in with a parole officer once a week, and that will be the extent of your sentence."

"Oh, thank you," Tansy said, and the other ladies nodded their heads.

"Keep in mind, that's what he's going to ask for," the president said. "Nothing is set in stone, and I can't make any promises.

"Now, as for you, young man." President Adams shook his finger at Ren. "Your aunt and her friends made me think a little harder than I'm used to, but you?" He looked down at his desk again. "You really muddied the waters."

"I wasn't trying to complicate things," Ren said.

"What do you mean?" Ida Mae asked.

"Well, do you want to tell her, or should I?" President Adams asked Ren.

"Let me." Ren turned to Ida Mae. "I met with Bishop Sylvester and President Adams last night and asked about serving a mission."

Ida Mae startled. "You want to serve a mission?"

Arlette piped up. "I didn't think you could," she said bluntly.

"I'm not bad, Arlette. I'm just drawn that way."

"What's he talking about?" Arlette whispered to Eden.

"It's a movie quote. I'll explain it later," Eden returned.

President Adams held up a hand. "We talked with Ren quite extensively, and we both feel that after six months of regular church attendance, he'll be ready to serve a mission. He'll squeak in just under the age limit. His tithing is paid in full, he has nothing to confess to Church leadership—he just needs to get himself active again."

Ida Mae blotted her face with a tissue. Her heart was so full, it almost hurt. "I'm glad," she managed to choke out.

Ren leaned over and kissed her on the check. "Me, too."

"Plus," the president continued, "that six-month delay will give Ren time to finish his own community service. That is, if he puts in about two hours a day, and if the judge agrees."

That reminded Ida Mae. "What will happen to Nick?"

"They don't know yet. It's only been a few days since this whole thing hit the fan, and they're working through the evidence. I talked with Captain Wright, and he's pretty sure Nick will have to spend some time in jail. But as he'd had a change of heart and was coming for help, and as he testified against the men behind the whole thing, he'll be able to plea bargain for a lesser sentence."

"And Mary?"

"We don't know yet. But whatever they decide, the stake will step in and take care of the home and children. Never fear."

"Maybe that could be part of our community service," Ida Mae said.

President Adams nodded. "I think that would be a wonderful idea." He reached into his desk drawer and pulled out an envelope. "There's one more matter to discuss."

Ida Mae took the envelope and opened it. Inside was a letter, promising the delivery of a check for ten thousand dollars, due to arrive in a few weeks.

"What's this?" she asked, completely confused.

"That's reward money for bringing down the drug ring," President Adams explained. "The police asked me to pass it on, to divide between you."

"But we can't accept this," Ida Mae said, and everyone else nodded their heads in agreement.

"I think you should," President Adams said. "Ren's going to have mission expenses, you know."

"I have a life insurance policy from my mother," Ren told him. "I think spending it on a mission would be the best possible use."

"Well, then, Ida Mae, why don't you use that money to go pick up Ren from his mission, wherever he serves," the president suggested.

Ida Mae nodded thoughtfully. "I think I could do that. As long as the other Secret Sisters come with me."

"It's a deal," Tansy said.

Epilogue

Mr. Phillips and the other men who ran the warehouse confessed to setting up the drug ring and to hiring James Jeffries to be the courier for the ring, paying off the employees who had been roped into service. But when James got a little too big for his britches and wanted a larger piece of the pie, that's when he took his drive into the river, his brake line having been cut. No money—wet or otherwise—was found in the car at all. Ricky imparted this news reluctantly—he couldn't get over the idea that Ida Mae had brought down a drug ring, of all things, and she couldn't get over how fun it was to make him feel sheepish. She pressed him for information on Nick and Mary's sentences, but he couldn't divulge anything he didn't know himself.

"For crying out loud, Ida Mae, these things take time!" he told her. "As soon as I know anything, I'll tell you. But it's not an overnight decision."

Brother Mangrum's plea bargain worked, and the Secret Sisters cheerfully fulfilled their six months of community service, finding it to be similar to their work in the Relief Society Presidency. Very little had changed in their daily routine, except they no longer had to coordinate visiting teaching, arrange for substitute teachers, or choose the hymns to be sung with each lesson.

Ren put in his papers and got his mission call to serve in Mexico. Ida Mae pressed her copy of his assignment into her journal, running her fingers across the words. She couldn't wait to see what kind of missionary he'd be, and to start sending him care packages. She made a mental note to check international shipping rates on cases of mayonnaise.

Sneak Preview

Ida Mae Rides Again

Book Two
The Secret Sisters Mysteries

Chapter 1

Ida Mae stepped back and surveyed her freezer with satisfaction. It took her all morning, but she had replenished her stock of cranberry cookies and whole wheat bread. She had also frozen twelve single-serving lasagnas, four bowls of soup, and two sweet and sour chicken dishes. Cooking for one was definitely different than cooking for a household, but when she froze the extra servings, she could go for days without having to actually spend time in the kitchen. She felt like such a rebel.

She glanced at the clock. Tansy would be coming over in about ten minutes, and she was sure to want some fresh warm bread once she caught a whiff. Ida Mae thought for a moment. She had some freezer jam in the outside unit—just the thing to serve with the bread. But as she descended the steps from her kitchen to the garage, she lost her balance. For a moment she thought she'd be all right, but then she fell to the hard concrete floor in an ungraceful heap.

The words that sprang to her mind at the sudden pain weren't befitting a former Relief Society president, but she thought them anyway. She figured the Lord would understand. She hadn't felt such pain in her life, not even in labor—of course, she'd had her children in the age when women were totally knocked out to give birth. She didn't remember much of anything from those days.

She lay there for a moment, trying to take a deep breath. When she finally managed to raise her head, she could see that her left ankle was twisted at an odd angle.

Great. Just great.

Her phone was at least twenty feet away, and she couldn't get up at all. She didn't know what she was going to do.

"Ida Mae?" Tansy's cheerful voice rang through the house. "Ida Mae, are you home?"

"I'm out here, Tansy," Ida Mae called. "In the garage."

Tansy stepped through the door. "Ida Mae!" She clutched the doorframe, her face pale. "Are you all right? Speak to me!"

"I already did speak to you, remember?" Ida Mae was so relieved at Tansy's appearance, she was ready to forgive nonsensical babbling, but some things were just self-explanatory.

"How long have you been out here?"

"Just a few minutes."

"Well, thank goodness for that. Now, let's see." Tansy grabbed a coat from off the hook by the door and draped it over Ida Mae's curled body. "Should we call the ambulance, or do you think you could get in the car?"

Ida Mae thought about it for a minute. A trip to the hospital was definitely in order, but she didn't know if her insurance would cover the ambulance ride. "Let's try the car," she said at last.

Tansy placed a call to the hospital to let them know Ida Mae was coming. Thankfully, the hospital had added another wing in the last year, so they should be able to treat Ida Mae there without having to transport her to Salt Lake City. She could hardly bear the thought of a long drive—just going to the hospital here in Omni would be hassle enough.

"Just think of it this way," Tansy said. "You're already in the garage. A few more feet, and you'll be at the car."

Ida Mae pressed her lips together. She supposed that was a blessing, although she did have the overwhelming compulsion to strangle Tansy with her own purse strap.

That was the pain talking.

Tansy opened the back door of Ida Mae's car. "Let's have you crawl in here and lie down," she said. "Oh, you have a stick shift."

Ida Mae hadn't really thought about it, but yes, she did have a stick shift. "Can you drive one?"

"Well, I've never done it, but I'm willing to give it a try," she said. "Unless you want to use my car. I could pull it up the driveway, but you'd have a lot farther to crawl."

Ida Mae weighed her options. Should she crawl a couple of feet and put her life in the hands of a woman who might end up driving her into a tree, or should she crawl twenty or thirty feet to get into a different car with the same woman? The choice was fairly obvious.

Gritting her teeth, she pulled herself onto her knees. The pain shot up her leg and into her hip, taking her breath away. Sweat broke out in beads across her forehead.

"You can do it, Ida Mae," Tansy said, looking like a sixty-year-old cheerleader.

Ida Mae grasped the doorframe and pulled herself up on her good foot, then crumpled down the length of the back bench. Tansy helped tuck her feet up on the seat and closed the door, then got in on the driver's side.

"Okay, now what do I do?"

At least one good thing came out of the drive to the hospital. Ida Mae was so intent on keeping Tansy from stripping the gears, bouncing like a bunny through the intersection, and going over the guardrail that the focus was taken off the pain in her foot.

They came to a screeching halt at the emergency room doors ten life-threatening minutes later, and Ida Mae said a silent prayer of thanks.

"That was fun!" Tansy said, turning around in the seat to look at Ida Mae. "Now, you sit tight. I'm going to go in and get one of those cute orderlies to bring a wheelchair out here."

Ida Mae had never before stopped to contemplate the physical appearance of the orderlies at the hospital, but when one did come out with a wheelchair, she had to admit, he looked pretty good— like an angel of mercy, swooping down to deliver her from Tansy's grasp.

Eden was late for her job at the Salt Lake Sentinel. She walked out of the funeral home sedately, but broke into a trot when she reached the parking lot, throwing another glance at her watch. She hadn't meant to leave so late, but she got caught up in the service and lost track of time.

She pulled into a fast food restaurant and changed in the bathroom, shoving her dress and heels into her duffel bag. She grabbed a sandwich and was on her way in no time, but then immediately got caught in a traffic snarl on I-215.

"Drat," she muttered, looking around for a way to exit. There wasn't one. She drummed her fingers on the steering wheel as the long string of cars inched forward, the other drivers looking as irritated as she was. Finally she saw an opening and took it, gunning her engine and zipping across, praying no one would hit her. They didn't, but they certainly did honk.

"Sorry," she called out, taking the exit. She wove through the back roads and pulled into her parking spot twenty minutes late. Maybe if she snuck in, no one would notice.

That didn't work. Halfway across the lobby, she heard her name.

"Eden! Wait up."

She turned, not wanting to face her boss, and got her wish. It was Kevin, the cute crime reporter who occupied the cubicle next to hers. She glanced around, not seeing Mr. Cooper anywhere.

"He's at lunch," Kevin said, correctly interpreting her look of worry. "So, I hear you took the morning off to go to a funeral. Are you okay?"

Eden cocked her head. It wasn't *her* funeral—of course she was okay. Then she realized what he meant. "I'm fine, Kevin. It wasn't for anyone I knew."

"What?" He followed her down the hall toward their cubicles. "You went to a funeral, but you didn't know the person who died?"

"Yeah, I know it sounds a little crazy. But haven't you ever gotten so wrapped up in a story, you had to find out more, even though the article was already published?"

"I think we all do."

"Well, it's no different for me. I see information come across my desk, and I try to condense someone's whole life into one short obituary, and I can only hope I did it right. Sometimes I like to see how close I came."

"You mean, you make a habit of this funeral-going thing?"

She shrugged. "Only once or twice a month, and generally just to the ones held on my days off. Today was an exception."

He shook his head. "I knew you were quirky, but I didn't know you were a funeral crasher." They reached her desk, and she bent to tuck her purse under the cabinet. "So, have you ever been proven wrong about a person?"

"Sure, of course. You know how it is—the bereaved turns in their copy, I clean it up, and it goes to press with all sorts of glowing praise heaped on it. Then at the funeral, I overhear that the louse cheated at cards and stole candy from babies. But you're supposed to print what they send, you know?"

"But how does that make you feel, when all the world—well, all the subscribers—see this marvelous write-up, but it's not true?"

"Can you imagine an obituary that was really accurate?" Eden held her hands up in front of her, pretending to read a newspaper. "He was killed in a motorcycle accident that he wouldn't have been in if he hadn't been stinkin' drunk and out seeing his girlfriend on the sly. Police say if he'd been smart enough to wear his helmet, he probably wouldn't have died—although his wife says, 'Good riddance to him and his smelly socks.'" She lowered her arms. "It would make fascinating reading, but is that really what the family needs?"

"No, I guess not." He folded his arms and leaned against the dividing wall between her office and his. "Can I come with you sometime?"

She looked at him with surprise. "You want to crash a funeral with me?"

"Sure, why not? It sounds like fun."

She mulled that over. She'd already divulged far more than she'd intended—there was something about Kevin that just made her want to talk. That could be dangerous. "I guess," she said. "I'll let you know the next time I go."

"How do you pick them? Do you just flip through the stack, close your eyes, and jab your finger?"

She really didn't want to tell him, but again, his undeniable charm worked its magic. "I go to the ones that make me cry."

"Come again?"

Dang it, if those brown eyes made him look any more like a puppy . . . "While I'm writing up the obituaries, some of them make me cry. Those are the ones I get curious about."

Kevin shook his head again, and she wondered what kind of sarcastic comment he was getting ready to make. She could take him down in the sarcasm department any day—it was her specialty.

"You're something else, Eden," he said, catching her off guard. And then he disappeared into his own cubicle, and she heard the sound of quick typing a moment later.

At least one of them was getting back to work— she had to pull her brain around to the task at hand. She hoped Mr. Cooper wouldn't figure out how late she'd been.

About the Author

Tristi Pinkston is the author of four published novels: Nothing to Regret, Strength to Endure, Season of Sacrifice, and Agent in Old Lace. While historical fiction is her first love, and indeed, she has been critically acclaimed for it, she has enjoyed her recent foray into contemporary mystery and plans to write several books in this genre.

Tristi is a popular and regular presenter at the annual LDStorymakers Writers Conference, and has presented at numerous other conferences and workshops, often sharing her unique sense of humor and love of life with her listeners. She also gives presentations on the importance of literacy. She maintains that life without books equals a painful death, and rather than see anyone subjected to such a fate, would rather talk with them about how to bring good literature into their lives.

Tristi enjoys good movies, taking long naps, scrapbooking (when she has the time, which isn't often) and teaching other writers how to dig within themselves for the very best they have to offer. She has been a much sought-after media reviewer for the past five years and blogs regularly about her book and movie finds.

Tristi and her husband, Matt, have been married for fourteen years and together they have four adorable, smart, talented, creative, home schooled, wonderful children who keep them busy and running in circles most of the time. They live in the Rocky Mountains.

You can visit Tristi's website at:

www.tristipinkston.com

and her blog at:

www.tristipinkston.blogspot.com

You can also write her very complimentary letters and send them to:

Tristi@tristipinkston.com